LIFE CROSSINGS

Learning to Look Both Ways

✠ ✠ ✠

TIM SEEBER

WESTBOW
PRESS®
A DIVISION OF THOMAS NELSON
& ZONDERVAN

WestBow Press books may be ordered through booksellers or by contacting:

WestBow Press
A Division of Thomas Nelson & Zondervan
1663 Liberty Drive
Bloomington, IN 47403
www.westbowpress.com
844-714-3454

ISBN: 978-1-6642-3155-9 (sc)
ISBN: 978-1-6642-3154-2 (hc)
ISBN: 978-1-6642-3156-6 (e)

Library of Congress Control Number: 2021908050

Print information available on the last page.

WestBow Press rev. date: 05/04/2021

To Roxanne, Suzie, Katie,
Mark, Chris, and Abby.

INTRODUCTION

✠ ✠ ✠

FOR TOO LONG, I WAS so busy and productive I didn't take enough time to reflect on the living that surrounded me. I am learning to pay better attention to much of what would be easy to miss.

As a Christian, this fits well with our call to be selfless rather than selfish and to look to those around us rather than be preoccupied, as if we are the most important person alive. My education gave me many of the right answers, but it took years to learn these were merely a starting place for life's continuing education. Faith is more than knowing the right answers; it's understanding how those answers are translated into living.

Photography has become a favorite hobby. As I learned to develop film in the darkroom and manipulate images with computer software, I found myself paying more attention to the content of my pictures. They became art rather than snapshots, and I realized they had captured more color, contrast, and life than I had seen when taking the pictures. In time, this helped me slow down and pay better attention to what I often missed at first glance. In turn, that has helped me learn not to miss subtle, important life lessons that are always around me.

Stories are a verbal form of art and stir up the imagination and memories of all who hear them. Like a photograph or painting, they evoke emotions and create a bond that allows for further dialogue and understanding. I am a husband, father, and pastor who has learned through the help of family and friends that sermons and articles that included real-life stories had more impact than those that did not. Having been encouraged to share such stories in a book, I am doing just that—sharing stories that have helped me to grow.

DADDY, PLEASE SAY NO

✠ ✠ ✠

THE FIRST CHILD IS ALWAYS an experiment in parenting. My daughter, Katie, was a wonderful teenager full of energy and life, and sometimes she just knew how to push my buttons. She was in high school when her mother died, and I struggled with being a single parent. One night, in her senior year, she called from a party. "Dad," she said, "I know curfew is at eleven o'clock, but can I stay out until midnight?" I always hated those calls and was never comfortable negotiating on the phone. My first reaction was to just say, "No way!" but I was trying to keep from butting heads and was trying to be as sensitive as her mom always had been.

So, I instead I embarked on a rambling lecture about agreed-upon rules, why they were important, and how when I was her age, I walked twelve miles to school in the snow and didn't whine about it. (Well, the last part really wasn't really part of the conversation, but you get the gist.) Anyway, I started to explain why it wasn't fair to make an exception and why we had agreed on eleven o'clock. You know the drill and have been on both sides of that conversation. She asked again, "Dad, can I stay until midnight?"

I started another train of my world-famous logic that certainly would convince her of the error of her ways. She interrupted me. "Dad, I don't want a story; can you just say yes or no?" So I said no. And I felt like I was the worst dad in the world. My guilt increased when I heard her yell to her friends, "My dad says I have to come home!"

Around eleven o'clock, I heard the front door open and anticipated a pouting young lady. I geared up for a battle. Instead, she gave me a hug and said, "Thank you, Dad."

I was caught off guard and wondered out loud, "You really didn't want to stay out till midnight, did you?"

She said, "No. I wanted to leave, but I wanted my friends to think you were making me come home. It's easier for me that way. My friends just don't understand."

And another lesson was learned by a father-in-training. Some surprises are more welcome than others. But that night, she, and not her father, was the teacher. It has reminded me how a baby in a manger became the most wonderful teacher of all! We are parented by a God of grace who has never wavered in his love and isn't afraid to share with us the goals, vision, and guidance for what life in the family of God is all about. Instead of a long story, he came in the flesh to do what we couldn't and empower us to do more than we thought possible.

How blessed we are that our God found a way to counteract the power of sin and death when he could have found an easier and less painful choice and simply looked the other way. How we live in response is our celebration of God's remarkable gifts of grace to a broken world.

Don't ever be afraid to just say no or yes when the motive is love!

HITTING THE SNOOZE BUTTON

✟ ✟ ✟

THERE IS NO MORE UNWELCOME surprise than a sudden noise from an alarm clock when you're warm and cozy and deep in blissful sleep. And so our choice is often to disregard the alarm and just hit the snooze button. I mean, that's what it's there for, right?

I can remember many times when I wasn't quite ready for sleep to end and I pounded that little button on my clock radio and rolled back over for another fifteen minutes of sleep. It seemed like a gift—more sleep! What a marvelous invention. But as I think about it, there are only two reasons for a snooze button. The first is that I am not getting enough sleep. And the second is that I don't want to face what I'm waking up to. So, the snooze button is really an avoidance button, an escape. If I go to bed when I should, I never need to snooze. When I'm in a positive frame of mind and eager for the gift of a new day, I don't want to snooze.

So, now I am conflicted about the gifted button called snooze, and I wonder whether it is just another crutch or an escape I can do better without. I mention this because when we started Lent, we set our alarm clocks of faith for Easter. When that joyful noise arrives, will we wake or snooze? Will we be so tired of daily routines that we won't join in celebration, or will life's tough stuff (that we keep trying to hide from) cause us to miss the joy of Easter's new day?

Didn't Easter wake the world from sleepy avoidance of reality with a simple message? Wake up! Open your eyes! It is a brand-new day filled with the joy of never-ending love! You never need to hide or hit the snooze button again.

Actually, every morning is a new Easter, a gift—another day blessed by the miracle of life and the victory over Satan's darkness. Every morning, we begin with the choice of jumping out of bed and celebrating what God will do next or crawling back into our cocoon of darkness and selfish escape. Lent is a marvelous gift of remembering the darkness of sleep and how Easter brings the powerful gift of a bright, warm, joy-filled, sunny new day.

As we celebrate Easter this year, maybe we should fill the sanctuary with alarm clocks rather than lilies and set them to all go off at once. And then we can shout together, "He is risen! No more snooze button!" (Well, maybe not, but it is something to think about.) And maybe tomorrow when you can't decide whether to snooze or not, you should think about Easter!

A CERAMIC SANTA

✠ ✠ ✠

THINK ABOUT CHRISTMAS ROUTINES, WHY they are important to you and what they say to family and friends. My great-grandparents did *not* decorate a tree until Christmas Eve, and then they celebrated Christmas for the next twelve days. We have gotten used to celebrating early (beginning with the post-Thanksgiving sales) and are ready to end our joy on Christmas Day. Advent challenges us to wait.

Why is it so difficult to wait? What do we miss by not waiting, and what might we gain if we did? Thinking about how our Black Friday–induced shopping frenzy overpowers the true meaning of the season, I remembered a cheap gift from years ago. One of the members of my first congregation gave me a gift of a ceramic Santa kneeling in front of the baby Jesus. To be honest, I wasn't very appreciative. It seemed tacky and a commercialization of the Bethlehem miracle. And so I showed how religious I was by preaching a sermon about how Santa had invaded Christmas.

In many ways, that is true, but Santa hasn't done it—we have. And because this holy night has become so commercialized, it is easy to pick on easy targets like a ceramic Santa. That beats admitting I really am too busy for Advent and am worn out by December 26 because of all the pre-Christmas noise, guilt, planning, and pressure. (We always feel better when we deflect our guilt on someone else!) Anyway, over the years, I started thinking about that Santa kneeling at the manger in a different way. Maybe, just maybe, I had missed the point! It wouldn't be the first time, and it won't be the last!

Rather than being another cheap and commercial Christmas ornament, most likely its intent was to proclaim that even Santa must kneel before the manger. And if you take the time to learn the story of St. Nicholas, who became the model for Santa, that might provide some other interesting thoughts. The real issue is how we decide to use or misuse the season.

Maybe Santa kneeling in front of a baby is one of the best reminders I was ever given of the appropriate posture for this most holy season. As we prepare to celebrate the birth of a baby, which you must agree is an amazing shape for the God of creation to assume, can we not take time to reflect upon the true nature of what we are preparing to celebrate rather than getting dragged along with the teeming and huddled masses of people who are more into tradition than a willingness to kneel at a manger? For me, this simple image of Santa kneeling has become a reminder of the appropriate posture I should assume, even in the midst of my earthly preparations and joy. What about you? When will you be ready to kneel at the manger?

MILITARY HONORS

✠ ✠ ✠

MY FATHER GRADUATED FROM THE US Military Academy and served as a career officer in the army. He attained the rank of full colonel and was selected for promotion to general but retired because he had the opportunity to go to work for the mission board of the Lutheran Church. Before there was even the thought of a movie by that name, he was already an officer and a gentleman. More importantly, he was a loving father, a faithful husband, and a man of faith.

When he died, he was buried with full military honors at Arlington National Cemetery. That included a band, a platoon from the Third Infantry, a caisson that carried his flag-draped casket, and a riderless horse with boots facing backward in the stirrups (just like the movies!).

It was a somber parade on an appropriately rainy day but one filled with much pride and love. The riderless horse symbolizes a rider who will ride no more. Because my dad's class at West Point was the last to receive cavalry training, and because he served with the Eighth Cavalry in Korea, a riderless horse will always be a powerful image for me. As I thought about the impact of that horse, I was reminded of an image that is so much more important in our lives of faith—an empty cross.

In Jesus's day, the cross was constructed for capital punishment—to carry a guilty body to death. Jesus of course didn't deserve that fate but accepted it on our behalf, to erase our guilt and destroy the finality of death. Every time we lift that empty cross, we rejoice that it will never be mounted again; it will stand empty forever! Many nonbelievers ridicule Christians for such a gruesome image, yet we know it is the most joyful and loving image we have been given!

Christ lived to make the cross his Messianic throne, using that tree of death as a place to miraculously restore new life to a fallen world. Just as an empty horse symbolizes a fallen raider, so the empty cross proclaims that a sacrifice undertaken once, for all, will never need to be repeated. Daily, that cross becomes a loving reminder of God's love for us and the undeserved sacrifice Jesus undertook to set us free.

On the other hand, a *crucifix* (a cross with a crucified Jesus on it) emphasizes his suffering and keeps us from forgetting the pain and agony of his gift of love. But more powerful is the empty cross, because it announces that the sacrifice is over forever! Christ's suffering has ended, and (like the tomb) the cross will never be mounted again! As images go, there is nothing quite like that empty cross. Every time you see that image, remember the victory that it symbolizes and the love with which it was embraced.

Because of Dad's faith, a riderless horse was not only a symbol of his commitment to his career but also an image much like the cross. For Jesus will never need to hang on a cross again, and because of his sacrifice, we have been set free.

HOBOS FOR LUNCH

✠ ✠ ✠

MY GRANDFATHER WAS A LUTHERAN pastor. He grew up in
the early 1900s and, after graduating from the seminary in St. Louis,
served a congregation in Little Rock, Arkansas, during the final years of
the Great Depression. I know that he and Grandma didn't have much
money—ever! But that never kept them from being who they couldn't
help but be.

I'll never forget a story that Grandma told me about those difficult
years during the Depression. She told me that Grandpa always walked
home for lunch. Along the way, he had to cross the railroad tracks that
separated downtown from the neighborhood where the church and their
home were located.

Grandma said that she quickly became accustomed to setting an
extra plate for lunch, despite their own lack of food. The reason she did
that was that Grandpa would wander through the train yard on his way
home, looking for someone who might need a meal. She said there were
many days he would bring a "hobo" home for lunch.

As I think about that story, I am struck by the reality that there
is nothing such a guest could have offered in return, except the
opportunity for my grandparents to be the hospitable servants that

they were committed to be. They didn't give to receive, so there was no other motive than faithful love. And yet I can't help but think that such giving gave much to them in return.

Hospitality is an act of love that can happen only when someone makes a practice of serving others. When it becomes a lifestyle, amazing things happen. Any love involves risk. Hospitality is a mighty risk, as one must drop barriers by inviting others to share in your life. As we serve others, we open ourselves to the potential of being served. An important thing that happens, should any of us open our door to others, is that fresh air from outside replaces the same old stale air that surrounds too much insider living.

And the risk of being hospitable yields rewards beyond what ever could have been imagined. I don't know all the conversations that my grandparents had with their guests, but I do know that their actions influenced many others, such as me! Hospitality is like a gift that can be opened twice, just like an open door that not only allows someone in but enables those inside to go out.

Remember, just as you love to be invited in, sometimes it is you who needs to be willing to open a door to those who are out. And not with the hope that you will surprise others but that you are open to being surprised by the many ways that God's love touches you!

DOG LESSONS

✠ ✠ ✠

I REMEMBER A WINTER WHEN it snowed hard and often. After several weeks of snow, the drifts got higher and higher. There is always something refreshing in a snowfall! And the moon seems so much brighter when reflecting off the snow! But that year's abundance of snow made for a major inconvenience for our two dogs, especially the shorter one.

When we had about fifteen inches of snow on the ground, I finally relented and went out in the backyard and shoveled paths for the dogs. It was the only way our beagle could move through the snow. But I wondered how my life got to the point of having to create pathways for dogs! It took a long time, and after every major snow, I had to redo the paths.

Those pathways were like tunnels that provided an adventure for the dogs and adequate space for them to make their daily deposits. It was actually amusing to watch as they got to that path farthest from the house, where the only thing visible was the beagle's tail pointed in the air, like a flag on the back of a dune buggy. Of course, Winston never thanked me for my effort, but all of life can be like that, more often than we would like to admit.

I did it because it needed to be done. (But I also know that a part of me felt badly for the dogs, and that was my motivation as well.) Every time I looked at those paths, I remembered what a pain it was to dig them out. But every time the dogs went out, I was also glad I had made the effort. Sometimes we do things not for rewards but because it is necessary or simply the right thing to do. And sometimes we do things for others because they are unable to do them for themselves.

Now, as I reflect, I wonder why I was motivated to go so far out of my way for dogs when sometimes it is difficult for me to make the same time for people. As I reflect on the pathways that were carved out for my life by parents, friends, and especially God, I am reminded that I have often used those paths without paying attention to who has done that for me, and I have often forgotten to say thanks. I surely can't expect such a response from my dogs, but there should be no excuse for me to take such acts of love for granted. (And besides that, who would have thought my dogs would become my teachers?)

THE CHRISTMAS ANGEL

✠ ✠ ✠

WE ALL HAVE SPECIAL PEOPLE who cross paths with us in life. As a pastor, I am blessed with many such opportunities, because my life is spent with so many different people. There was one elderly woman in our congregation who might have been the gentlest, sweetest, and most quietly joyful person I have ever known. No matter what, she was in a good mood, and no matter how ill, she always smiled. Her last Christmas Eve was spent in a hospice facility.

She had lived ninety-eight wonderful years and outlived all her family and friends. She was dying. As I went to visit her on Christmas Eve, I was filled with sorrow and sadness that she was spending her last Christmas all alone. She knew she was preparing for her heavenly reunion. I will never forget entering her room that that morning. As always, I was greeted by her smile.

But before I could even say hello, she broke the silence with these words: "Oh, it is so good to see you, Pastor. Christmas Eve, as you know, is my most favorite day!" She knew she was close to death yet had the appearance and energy of a little child staring at a tree surrounded by gifts. Like a Christmas angel, she radiated joy and peace!

What a moment of humbling awareness it was for me as she gave more to me than I could have possibly given her. She wanted to talk about how she celebrated Christmas Eve as a child and as an adult and why this day was her favorite. And so she talked, and laughed, and talked some more. I sat at her feet and listened. As I reflected on what she shared about the many Christmas joys and the peace she felt, I couldn't help but see how (although alone) she felt anything but alone and was ready for what was coming next.

There was no fear, no regret, only the quiet peace of her smile and joy, which colored every word she whispered. In such a quiet setting, I could feel the presence of the baby Jesus, which couldn't have been heard in noise of the stores or traffic on that busy day! In the quiet of that place, all I could think was that was what it must have been like for Mary and Joseph on the first silent night.

With no distractions, one can only focus on the true gift of this Christmas Eve. What a gift! A baby who brings light to fill darkness with the gifts only God can give. I was so glad I had visited her. I had arrived thinking I was doing my duty as a pastor but found out that she had the jump on me and was doing hers. She wanted to share the joy of the baby Jesus and didn't want to be distracted by anything else.

What a soft, gentle, and quiet start to Christmas Eve. It might well have been my best Christmas Eve ever! I just love it when angels sing!

BARRY GORDY

✠ ✠ ✠

I SPENT MY LAST TWO years of high school living in the suburbs of Washington, DC. It was the late 1960s, and Motown was the only music any of us listened to. The genius behind that sound was a man named Barry Gordy. We visited the house in Detroit where Motown began. During the tour, we were told that in 1959 Gordy borrowed $800 to buy the house in Detroit to make records. Seven years later, Motown was worth $20 million.

How did he manage to find Diana Ross, Martha Reeves, Jackie Wilson, Smokey Robinson, David Ruffin, the Temptations, and all the others? Well, the surprise was that he didn't find them. They brought each other to him, one at a time. His first singer told him about her cousin. When she made a record, she told him about friends who had a group. That group knew another group. As success followed success, other groups came and wanted to join the Motown label. And that is how $800 turned into a $20 million company in seven years.

Now, the church is a different organization but has always grown in similar fashion. Peter and Paul were so excited about Easter they did all they could to bring others into that same relationship of saving love. One at a time. Day after day. Strategies and planning have their place, but success in the church always boils down to the passion of love in relationships and the willingness to bring a friend or invite a cousin or two. That is how twelve disciples continued a movement begun by Jesus that has touched billions of lives and continues to change lives two thousand years later.

We are members of the church because of relationships and the living Word. None of our congregations exist to make millions of records or dollars, but we do have a product that has changed our lives. And he is a gift to be shared freely for all! As part of Christ's body (the church), we exist to celebrate, nurture, and share the faith. That is the business of being a disciple.

Motown's success was a result of every singer pitching in. When not singing, each would sweep floors, answer phones, or practice their gifts. Should it be any different for us? We aren't brought into the church to sit around but to pitch in and use our gifts so the kingdom grows! Jesus didn't just die for me but for *all*. How will all know if each of us isn't joyfully sharing Good News every day? If Motown could use such a one-at-a-time technique to attract singers and make records, why can't we use that technique for a grander and more joyful goal? One by one, word by word, we grow!

WRONG NUMBER!

✠ ✠ ✠

HAVE YOU EVER HAD ONE of those mornings when you overslept and had to fly out of the house so you wouldn't be late? There are few things more upsetting than oversleeping before a final exam, or an important meeting, or having to lead worship. One morning, my alarm did not go off. I woke up twenty minutes before a scheduled meeting and rushed to get ready. I couldn't figure out why the alarm had not gone off but didn't have time to figure it out. Roxanne didn't have to go to the office as early as I did that day, so I set the alarm for thirty minutes later and headed off to get Abby to school and me to church.

When I got to church, I kept worrying about the alarm clock and decided to call Roxanne to make sure she was awake for work. The phone rang about six times, and then it was picked up. The conversation went something like this: "Are you up?" I asked.

In return, I got a sleepy reply, "Yes … well, I am now!"

I said, "Good, because I had trouble with the alarm this morning and was afraid you might not get up."

There was a pause, and then a question followed. "Who is this?"

I said, "Your husband."

"Oh," she answered, "this is Kelly!" (Now I *do* know my wife's name, and it isn't Kelly—oops!)

"Sorry," I said. "Guess I had a wrong number, but I'm glad you are up!"

She laughed and hung up. How uncomfortable when you call someone and find out you aren't talking to whom you thought you were? Or how do you feel when someone greets you on the street and starts talking as if she is your best friend and you can't remember if you have ever met that person or not?

These things do happen, and it is never an easy time as we try to figure out where we heard that voice or saw that face before. How would you feel if you jumped into a prayer only to learn God's didn't know who you were or remember the sound of your voice? Wow! That would be scary!

Thankfully, no matter how far we stray or how often we are too distracted to spend time in prayer, God knows our name and is present in our lives. But why would we ever do that to God? If we are loved so much, shouldn't we check in more often and more intentionally? After all, there might be something God has to share with us. Think of all we would miss if God simply got a busy signal. Don't stay distant from someone who is always by your side!

HIDING IN THE CHURCH

✟ ✟ ✟

WHILE SERVING A CONGREGATION IN Toledo, there was a time when the local newspaper carried story after story of bizarre events happening in or around local farms. Several farmers had found animals butchered in strange ways. Bonfires were set in a pastures late at night, where trespassing was obviously going on. No one was sure what was going on and how much concern there should be. There were rumors of satanic rituals and devil worship. The stories continued for several months.

One day, I received a phone call from one of our members who was a deputy sheriff. She explained she had gotten a tip on the police hotline from a woman who claimed to be a witch. She wanted to talk to the police about what she thought was really going on. Her only condition for talking to the police was that she insisted on being interviewed inside a church building.

(My thought, still today, is that if she thought God would keep her safe in one place, why not in other places? But, I imagine, once someone walks away from God, there isn't a lot of rationality and certainty about anything.) *You see, it isn't what we do that keeps us close to God, it is all about what God does to keep us close to him!* Anyway, that was not a request that had been covered in any of my seminary classes!

At first, I was worried about having a witch in our sanctuary and what would happen if anyone found out. After enough worrying, I decided to give the police a room (far away from my office) to do the interview, and they seemed happy with the results. I didn't meet this person or speak with her, but I thought a lot about it afterward.

So many seek to control God or protect themselves by the things they do. And many share the confusion that the church is a building, rather than people who have been changed by Christ and celebrate that grace by living in faith. Too many ignore God until they are in a panic. (But if God is part of everyday living, why would there ever need to be a reason to panic?) Many say, "I don't need the church to be a Christian," but unless one is part of the body of Christ and connected in a regular way to the hands and feet of Christ's body on earth, any building they are in is only a building!

Martin Luther wrote about this in his Small Catechism. He believed that it is not our own wisdom or actions that bring us to faith in Christ. Instead, God comes to us through his Holy Spirit. No matter how fervently we seek to reach God, it is in God's reaching into our hearts and minds that faith becomes the gift that it is. The world is full of evil as well as good. But there is only one God! If I trust in him more than anything else, then I have peace!

ROUGH RIDE AHEAD

✠ ✠ ✠

I REMEMBER A TURBULENT FLIGHT into Chicago when the pilot announced those dreaded words, "Fasten your seat belts. We're in for a rough ride. There's turbulence ahead." And boy was he right! What a rough ride it became!

For twenty minutes, we circled O'Hare, and the jet dropped, bumped, and bounced. All the while, we were totally surrounded by fog. I didn't know if we were at 15,000 feet or 500 feet. I kept expecting the plane to land, and then it would climb and bounce some more. That was more than disconcerting. It was scary! It was like that dark and stormy night when Jesus and his disciples were trapped on the lake in a terrifying storm. (Seems appropriate in our world, doesn't it?)

They kept rowing in the midst of a terrible storm, pulling hour after hour with heavy wooden oars. Because of wind and waves, they couldn't even tell if they were making headway. Seasick, worried, and full of apprehension, they suddenly saw Jesus standing next to the boat! (How could they not have been scared out of their wits?) And then he calmed both the storm and their fears.

His message was simply to trust him rather than their fear. And so Jesus, rather than the storm, became their focus. And they reached the other shore safely. Two points immediately come to mind. Even in their darkest moment, they were not alone! More importantly, Jesus brought them to the end of their journey. That dark and stormy night was brightened by Jesus's presence, and although the work was tiring, Jesus got them to the other side.

Do you think it is any different with us? How are you doing in your day-by-day walk with Jesus? Is it the darkness or the daylight that seems to preoccupy your steps? Many struggle with very difficult issues. Others are doing "just fine, thank you." Sometimes the roles are reversed. But always, it is good to remember this story and know that we never walk alone. Jesus will get us to the other side! The disciples could have been so distracted by their hard work they might have missed Jesus. They also could have decided it was their hard work that got them safely to the other shore.

Some want to wallow in the darkness of storms, while others pretend good weather and smooth sailing are deserved because *they are special*. But it is time to acknowledge reality. Life is filled with the brokenness of sin. God's love causes him to jump into our wind and waves, just as he did with those disciples. Faith calls us to keep eyes on his promise and presence, rather than the storms that surround us. There is such peace, even in the midst of a storm, knowing he is standing by our side. And how refreshing to realize he will also get us to the other side. So rather than allow storms to distract, remember how one day on a stormy lake, fear turned into faith.

BIG OR LITTLE MAPS?

✤ ✤ ✤

I GREW UP BEFORE TIMESHARES, cruise ships, and Disney World. Family vacations when I was a child meant driving cross country on two-lane roads in a station wagon full of kids and suitcases and no air-conditioning. Our family had five children, and so with suitcases, ice chest, and no room to squirm, such trips were anything but comfortable. But we didn't know any better and had no other choices, so we endured.

To show how little things could be so exciting, I remember when Dad would stop for gas, and my brother and I could go inside and grab a free road map for the state we were in! We would track our progress to see how far we had come and how far was still left to go. Later, on rainy days at home, we would pull them out to remember our trips and what had happened along the way.

Today's maps don't even bear a resemblance. They are simply directions or a partial view of the journey on a cell phone or screen on the dashboard. They get you to the next exit, but you only have a close-up view. Electronics are not helpful for looking over an entire journey in one glance. And if the power goes out or the computer has a glitch, there is no backup. Without a road map, you can easily get lost. Think about our faith journey as a lifetime cross-country trip.

We have a destination in mind. We need to find our way home and not get lost. The Bible is our driving instructions. And there are two ways to use those instructions. You can simply check a passage here and there or look up an answer for a specific question. This is like using a Garmin or asking Siri. It might show where you are now and the next turn but not how far you have come or what might be a couple hours or days down the road.

On the other hand, if the Bible is used as a complete unit (like a road map) from Genesis to Revelation, then no matter what text or book you are reading, it has context in terms of the entire map or Bible. My point is simply that you need to study the whole map rather than just trust that you can hunt and peck for single answers or an immediate turn in your progress. You cannot read Revelation without knowing what Genesis is about, and if you have not read the Prophets, you will miss much of the power of the Gospels.

The life of faith is a journey with incredible twists and turns, and holy scripture is God's tool to give directions and help assess where we have been and where we are going. Don't get lulled into thinking you can just turn on the biblical GPS when you are lost. Instead, become familiar with the whole message so if your power goes out, you have a resource to get you home! Think about it!

A DYING BIRD

✠ ✠ ✠

HAVE YOU EVER SEEN A bird die? What I mean is, have you ever watched a bird just fall down and die? OK, I found a dead parakeet in a cage once and have had birds fly into the grill of my car, but I had never seen a bird just naturally die until a few days ago. I was on my early-morning walk, trying to get the cobwebs out of my head and erasing the dreams from the previous night. Suddenly there was a whoosh, and I caught a sense of motion. A shape passed just to my right and thumped on the grass.

I was startled. *What was that? What almost hit me? What is going on?* I turned, looked down, and there was a dove, lying on its back! Its feet reached straight, its body was still, and its wings were folded. It was quiet. It was dead. I mean, it just fell out of the sky, landing on its back with no warning, no reason. It just dropped and landed with a thump. That was it.

No hawks overhead, nothing at all. It just lay there. I didn't know what to think. (Maybe I still don't.) It was unexpected. Its life ended with no fanfare, no noise, and no one to take credit. I am still trying to figure out what the significance of that moment was. (And maybe there was none.)

What does one do with something that can't be explained or has never been seen before? Sometimes experiences have no reason or explanation; they just are. We are so into control we always expect there is a reason, such as why we have a warmer summer or colder winter. We expect a logical reason for a friend who abandons a partner, a stranger who has no home, or why one child succeeds and another fails. We always want to explain, or blame, or understand.

I think it is about control, which is our tendency to want to be like God. We don't like mysteries or things that make us feel uncomfortable. And when something weird happens that we can't explain, I think that is why we are so bothered. Yet bad things happen to good people, and good things happen to bad people, and birds fall out of the sky for no reason. Ultimately, and with all things, we can either struggle with what we can't control or find peace in knowing God's presence and love will conquer even our lack of control. In such moments, what can we do but stand quietly and know that God is still God? In such awareness, there always comes peace!

LOVE BUGS

✠ ✠ ✠

IN THE LUTHERAN CHURCH, THE third year of seminary training was practical training in a congregation. The vicarage (or internship) was spent under the supervision of a seasoned pastor. My assignment was to be in a small congregation in Miami, Florida. I hooked up a trailer to my Chevy Vega and headed from St. Louis to Florida. It was a long drive, and when I was within a few hours of Miami and starting to feel as if the worst part of the trip was behind me, I had my first encounter with what the natives would later tell me were "love bugs."

It started with a few splats on my windshield, but within minutes, the windshield was coated with dead bugs. After a few miles, I ran out of windshield solvent and couldn't keep it clean. I had to slow down, as it was difficult to see. Every rest stop for the next hour would involve paper towels and soap to attempt to clean that sticky mess. My car was a solid mass of love bug carcasses. It amazed me that such tiny critters could make such a big mess!

As I reflect, I see this now as an appropriate parable for daily living. Think of emails that get sent without a second thought, or comments on Twitter and Facebook. As we hit "send," we don't think about how a word cannot be taken back and real damage can occur. How often have we shared a rumor with the caution, "Now, don't tell anyone else," as if that lessens the impact of our bug blast? And what about the consequence of repeated barbs that are whirring around the ears of others?

We don't mean to be hurtful, but once a word is spoken, it can remain just like the mess of bugs on the grill of a car. None of us feel such tiny conversations can ever be devastating to others. Yet, when the same words or rumors are passed on and multiplied as others pass them along, like thousands of tiny bugs, by the end of a day, a life can be transformed into an unbelievable mess. And much of what sticks to others can be hard to clean away.

St. Paul warned about the tongue being the most dangerous weapon in our arsenal. We know how we have been hurt and need to remember how similarly we can hurt others. Too often, a casual comment or a knee-jerk reaction seems like just a little thing to us. But seldom do we consider how difficult, harsh, and judgmental comments can stick to the life of another like bugs on a windshield. Remember, it doesn't take many bugs to make a big mess.

It reminds me of a memorable line in the Disney film *Bambi*. It was given by Thumper (the rabbit), who simply said, "If you can't say anything nice, don't say nothin' at all!" And that makes sense when you think about how difficult some messes can be to clean up.

FREQUENT FLYERS

✠ ✠ ✠

I RECENTLY JOINED THE FREQUENT flyer program at our garden center, which simply means every thirteenth bag of bird seed that I purchase is free. I never joined in the past, as I could not imagine how long it would take to use that much seed. Well, times have changed. I forgot to account for the needs of squirrels. We have more squirrels than birds, and they can empty feeders faster than I fill them.

Squirrels do need to eat, but I wonder about the need to subsidize the entire squirrel population of our neighborhood, so I have changed tactics. I purchased two new feeders that are supposedly squirrel proof. Sounds great! Except I think the birds are afraid of them because no one is eating seeds now. I never figured out how birds find feeders in the first place and assumed if I put them in the same location, birds would keep coming (as I know squirrels will.) But so far, it hasn't worked that way. The feeders must be intimidating (being a different shape and color), and I guess it will take birds a while to come back.

I guess that makes sense because I am the same way. Change is difficult, and sometimes different packaging or a different appearance can put me off. How often have you gone to buy a familiar food item, and even though it was in the same spot on the shelf, you couldn't find it because the box was a different color? I guess all living things have that in common.

People get used to certain appearances, sounds, or traditions and struggle with change. Guests and visitors show up who aren't familiar with the old feeders and so are not intimidated by the new. In fact, whatever is being offered as food right now is what has drawn them to a congregation in the first place. I imagine the point becomes our need to understand perspectives of one another. I have found that it takes a lot more seed to feed a few birds than it used to but have changed tactics to make sure the job gets done. There are never easy answers in life, but we do know that food is basic, and as long as we are faithful in feeding the flock, we are on the right track. With faith, it is the food and not the feeder that is most important. Feeders might change, but the Living Word of a risen Savior will nourish forever!

RUNAWAY KIDS

✠ ✠ ✠

MY INTERNSHIP WAS IN A small congregation on Highway US 1, on the north side of Miami, Florida. It was the main drag into the city. The congregation was named Bay Shore Lutheran and had only about ninety members. At the ripe age of twenty-four, I was the youngest in the church, except for the two children in our Sunday school. They were six and eight, a brother and a sister, who lived with grandma because dad was in prison and mom was an addict who lived on the streets. One day, I got a call from their social worker, who said the kids had run away from grandma, and she wondered if I would try to find them.

Right! I had been in Miami only a couple of months and barely knew how to get downtown. How in the world would I find them? Our church was on Biscayne Boulevard, across from warehouses and railroad tracks. To the south was a gated community with stone walls. To the north were old motels and a tiny neighborhood about three blocks by three blocks.

To make a long story short, I spent about three hours driving around any place along the bay were I could find grass and trees. And surprisingly, I did find these two kids, walking in a park next to the bay. Once my heart quit pounding, I took them back to my apartment, fed them a sandwich, and called their social worker. She came and took them back to grandma's house. My initial reaction was that it was just plain luck that allowed me to wind up in the same place at the same time as they did. I am even more amazed they didn't run away from me when I got out of the car and asked them if I could take them home. And I wasn't sure how they would feel going home, because their life wasn't that great. But they decided they were ready for a reunion with grandma.

The more I reflect on this, I know I didn't find them, but God led me to them, and them to me. That story reminds me that God shepherds and gathers more than we know, even as we wait for what comes next. We sometimes are so busy with our own fears or are enamored with our successes that we fail to see the hand of God in our daily living. It is hard to know what God controls, when God gets involved, and when he steps back, but I know he is always close by, and this day was a powerful reminder of that fact!

WELCOME HOME, DADDY!

☩ ☩ ☩

WHEN MY YOUNGEST DAUGHTER WAS in grade school, I was gone two days for a conference. Such events are the only time I am away from home and family. When I returned home, the first thing I noticed on our patio door was a message written by her using Magic Marker on the glass. It said, "Welcome Home, Daddy! Love, Abby." I let the message remain for months, and the welcome still worked every night when I came home.

It is great to feel unconditional love, right? I realize one of the blessings of the unfortunate losses my children have faced in their lives is there are some things they no longer take for granted. My oldest children lost their mom when she died at the age of thirty-seven. After I remarried and had another child, they lost their twenty-five-year-old sister to a sudden death a year after she had her first child. Because of such losses, my kids have been very quick to say, "I love you," daily and often.

As they have moved away to their own families, every phone call ends with "I love you," and what a welcome home that is! This has been a joy for Roxanne and myself as well, as we know now how important it is never to take each other or our kids for granted. Not that the rest of you don't do the same, but I am a slow learner, and often it is through hard knocks that I finally embrace what should have been obvious.

Anyway, it is special for us that such welcomes and goodbyes are standard fare. Our family is no better than any other, and we all have made our share of mistakes, but how neat to hear the songs of welcome and love every day! As I remember that "Welcome Home, Daddy" sign, I am also reminded of the signs that God places in our midst and how important it is to take advantage of them. Advent is one such sign that says, "Welcome home."

We like to think we are getting ready for Christmas, but Advent is God's way of getting us ready to be welcomed into our true home! That is what a baby in the manger and an empty tomb are all about. What a loving way God has come to us and left signs in the window, and in the streets, and in our hearts, saying, "Welcome home!" Don't miss the signs. And look for special times, such as the season of Advent, which is like a sign on the glass that calls us to get ready for God to welcome us again in such a special way!

EXPLAINING GOD

✛ ✛ ✛

ONE DAY, I WAS SITTING in my office at church and got a phone call from a lady I had never met. She said they were looking for a new church to worship in. And then, almost as an aside, she said, "Oh, and my husband is dying of brain cancer. Could you bring him Holy Communion?" I agreed, got directions, and headed to their house. She said she would leave us alone. And so I sat with a dying man I didn't know who had just had brain surgery.

In that moment, I was reminded of just how much I take for granted. The conversation was difficult, as he couldn't match words and thoughts in a meaningful way. I asked if he wanted Holy Communion. "What is Communion?" he asked. An assumption of mine had trapped me in a corner. I explained with good Lutheran words about God's grace, to which the man responded, "What is God? I think I remember that word, but I just can't remember what it means." How could I explain God when we each spoke a different language? We all operate with assumptions and comfort levels that can get in the way of ministry. I thought I had all the answers, and too often, others feel they have none. The truth is somewhere else.

Our easy assumptions and comfortable excuses are roadblocks to ministry. It is like fishing; unless you get your line in the water, there is no way you will catch any fish. Well, anyway, I was trapped with good stock answers that were in a language a man with a brain tumor couldn't remember. How could I explain *God* as if for the first time?

As I wondered what to say, I noticed him looking at his flower garden. Not knowing what else to try, I asked about the beautiful flowers. "Yes," he said, "we planted them this spring."

Picking up on his cue, I asked about the bird feeders next to the garden. "You must really enjoy feeding and watching the birds."

He smiled and agreed that he did. I continued, "God is the word we use to talk about *who* created your flowers and the sun and the beautiful birds you feed."

I didn't know what else to say. I hoped that by keeping it as simple as I could, with something familiar and in words he might understand, I might stumble into a way to share a word about the God who loved this man so much. And then his face broke into a smile of remembering. "Yes," he said quietly, "I do remember that word. God! Yes, I know God."

"He loves you very much," I said. And he nodded that he remembered that too. Sometimes God is easier to explain than we imagine, and when we slow down and watch and listen, he shows us a way!

TAILLIGHTS IN THE FOG

✠ ✠ ✠

I WAS BLESSED TO SPEND three of my elementary school years in Germany. My dad was in the army and, we lived in Giessen, Germany. Every Sunday, Dad and Mom would pile the family into our old Studebaker station wagon and drive forty-five miles to Frankfurt for worship. There was an American Lutheran congregation there, and it was a great trip because afterward we would stop somewhere for lunch (which was a rare treat for an army family with four kids and a not-too- generous salary to live on). After lunch, Dad and Mom would have decided on a new castle or small village to visit, so our stay there was full of neat surprises.

Another thing I remember quite vividly was winter weather. It was never terribly cold, but much of the winter was blanketed with thick fog—intense fog! We drove on the Autobahn (their version of our interstates), and that meant white-knuckle driving. There was no speed limit, and people drove the same speed no matter the weather. Even in the fog, no one slowed down but simply followed the taillights of the car in front of them. If you slowed down, you might get rear-ended, and there were no reflective lane markers like we are used to, so that seemed to be how everyone was able to stay on the road.

But if one is going to follow the light, in that or any similar situation, wouldn't it be more comforting if you knew that whomever you followed really did know the way? One season of the church year is called Epiphany, which remembers the journey of wise men following a star to find Jesus. The theme of Epiphany remembers Jesus is the light of an entire world. He is the light we follow, and we light a candle at baptism as a reminder to let his light shine!

We are used to following many lights. And often, we don't know where they are leading us. Some are from people who are going where we want to go. And some are from people leading us where we shouldn't go. But if Jesus is always the light, no matter how intense the fog or darkness, we will never get lost, and he will always lead us safely home.

COINCIDENCE OR FRUITS OF FAITH?

✠ ✠ ✠

SOMETIMES EVENTS OCCUR THAT APPEAR to be random. Yet faith causes us to consider whether there might be a different explanation. After World War II, the Lutheran Church Missouri Synod commissioned Pastor "Pedo" Meyer to be a missionary in China. Less than a year later, he, his wife, Lois, and their young child had to flee as Mao Tse-tung's revolution turned China upside down. They arrived in Japan in 1948. Rather than return to the US, they were asked to help other missionaries begin Christian congregations in Japan. That same year, a US Army lieutenant and his wife (my parents) were sent to Japan as part of the rebuilding after the war. The Seebers and Meyers (along with the other Lutheran missionaries) became a great support group for one another in a far-off land.

In 1950, war broke out in Korea, and my father was sent with the first group of troops into Korea. While Dad was in Korea, I was born in Yokohama. Thanks to Pastor Meyer, Mom had someone to drive her to the hospital (in an army jeep, no less!). My mother's name is Eunice. Dad and Mom asked Pedo's wife, Lois, to be my godmother. Mom's familiarity with the Bible made a connection with Paul's letter to Timothy where he mentioned Eunice and Lois as the mother and grandmother of Timothy. That convinced Mom to name me Timothy.

And so, Lois, Eunice, and Tim have been connected for all these years because Mao Tse-tung overthrew the government of China. The Meyers would continue as missionaries in Japan for another twenty years. As an adult, I have come to know my godmother and her husband, whom I claim as an honorary godfather. For me, the point of this memory is quite simple. Had it not been for a series of seemingly random events, a group of people (united in their faith) would never have met. How appropriate that the love of Jesus led Meyers to Japan and my parents to become involved in the Japan mission effort, and I wound up with a special godmother in the mix. Coincidence? I think not! It has more to do with the fruits that come from faith. Take time to prayerfully consider how God has brought about similar gifts in your lives!

THE WITNESS

✠ ✠ ✠

WHILE ATTENDING THE SEMINARY IN St. Louis, I had a part-time job in the branch of a local bank. It was a quiet, little bank on the edge of town. The job didn't interfere with classes, and I was able to graduate with no student loans. There was never any drama, until one day a woman came to my window and asked me to cash her check. Something just didn't feel right.

It was a substantial check, but she had no identification. As I started to question her, she ran and disappeared down the street. I called the police, describing her size, skin, hair color, the color of her dress, and her gold front teeth. Within thirty minutes, a police van pulled up, and I was taken outside to identify the woman. But inside the van was a man!

I didn't know what to do. The police opened a shopping bag they had found in his car with the dress and wig I remembered. The man said, "It wasn't me!" As he spoke, I saw the gold tooth and remembered his eyes and voice. My confusion was cleared up as I identified him. Later on, I would be called to serve as a witness at his trial.

A witness can only tell what they have seen or heard. So here is a question: What might others remember about you? What have they seen, and what have they heard? What would cause you to be recognized, and how would you feel about the description of your life and your actions? No matter what you think you can hide, you are memorable in different ways to different people. That guy thought he had a perfect disguise, except he forgot one distinguishing characteristic.

How often have we tried to hide behind excuses or denials even as we knew deep down that such disguises are only temporary? Before Jesus was arrested, he washed his disciples' feet. In the process, he made sure they watched and remembered what he was doing for them. Such servant love became the characterizing description of the flavor of his ministry in our midst. Just like his birth in a manger is the way we see how God humbled himself to help us identify with his love.

When others look at you, will they see God's love and the peace, which comes from faith, or will they see something else? It is your choice. Choose well!

ATHEIST CHURCHES

✠ ✠ ✠

I WAS INTRIGUED BY A news story about some atheists who had attended church and decided to begin atheist churches. (True story!) In the interview, they said they loved going to church but felt it was a shame it was based on something they didn't believe. In the article, I remember one of the founders saying he was intrigued by the neat stuff going on in churches, such as singing, fellowship, inspirational messages on self-improvement, and helping others.

So he and other atheists decided to begin churches of like-minded atheists so they could experience what nonbelievers typically miss out on. So, is the winning formula providing awesome programs and good feelings? Some Christians might agree, especially when faced with a culture that increasingly removes more and more of the moral and ethical underpinnings we have been so used to. (Sometimes it is hard to remember where all of that "moral stuff" came from!) Today's wisdom is that faith in God gets in the way of cultural improvement. But where do values come from if not a belief system bigger than you and me? Are they simply from consensus or the relativity that culture assigns at any moment in time?

On the other hand, why is it that churches are so good at what they do that nonbelievers want a piece of the action? Some focus on programs as a way to gather and reward, but we need to reflect upon why those church programs are there in the first place. As some atheists felt they were missing something, their assumption was it was about programs. In reality, what they were missing was what they had decided they didn't want in the first place: God. Forgiveness. Grace. Mercy. Peace. All defined and gifted by God, not by any human organization, government, or person. What we do when we gather together is in response to what God has already given—and so we respond!

It is much like a family; we don't share meals, protect children, or build homes to create family but because we *are* family. It is sad that some just don't get it. On the other hand, doesn't this remind us why we gather, not to take our time together for granted, and what we might offer to those who feel left out?

COCONUT THE DOG

✠ ✠ ✠

EVERY WEEK WITH DOGS IS an interesting week. One week was more interesting than most. Coconut (the dog) was recovering from ACL surgery. That meant no climbing and no jumping, and she could be outside only on a leash and only to take care of business. I had to carry her up and down steps. She was on meds that she refused to take, so the battle for getting each pill down was an ordeal, to say the least. Roxanne (the wife) injured her Achilles tendon and was in a cast and on crutches, unable to put any weight on the injured leg, so she and the dog turned our downstairs into a hospital ward. I was definitely feeling sorry for myself. Then it snowed. And the temperature dropped!

And then the dog stopped eliminating. I called the surgeon for the dog. Here is how that conversation went: "Take the dog's temperature." I asked how. He said, "Rectally." I asked him to repeat himself! He repeated the same thing! So, I thought, *Easy for you to say*. I did the only thing that seemed reasonable and called my regular vet and asked if they could take her temperature. And they did. Driving there, I remembered to pray, even for the dog! (By the way, if this canine temperature thing ever comes up for you, it is definitely a two-person job!)

So, what is the point? Coming back from the vet, I thought about all the people I had visited the past week. Some had faced surgery, were coping with chronic illness, or entering hospice care. Others struggled with terrible situations at home. As I drove, I remembered all of the joy and peace that I encountered in their faith-filled lives. Roxanne's pain had begun to subside, and she was starting to get around better, and the temperature check apparently convinced the dog to resume normal bodily functions.

As I arrived home, I had to admit there is nothing more peaceful than being outside at night, in the quiet of a new fallen snow. Florida might be warmer than Michigan, but a fresh snowfall is truly a beautiful and peaceful sight. It always amazes me how I can worry about stuff I can't control and forget to marvel at the miracles God daily and lovingly sends our way. Sometimes life is complicated, but if we pay attention, God always finds ways to remind us that we are not alone and, in the end, the really big stuff is already covered.

MY TWO DOGS

✠ ✠ ✠

WE HAVE TWO DOGS. BOTH were rescued. Coconut is our fluffy, white, medium-sized dog who had the run of the house for about nine years until we got our little beagle named Winston. Winston is still trying to figure out life in our household, and Coconut has become his tolerant big sister. Coconut always has a large rawhide chewy around, while Winston has not mastered the art of gnawing on such contraptions. Plus, those rawhides are almost as big as he is, so the effort would be futile.

One night, Winston tiptoed into the family room and sneakily (he thought) picked up Coconut's chewy right from under her nose. Slowly, he dragged it to his secret hiding place. Coconut just watched and then went back to sleep. If she could, I am sure she would have rolled her eyes. I mention this only as it is interesting to watch how dogs interact and either do or don't become part of a pack or a community. Each has a different personality, yet they find ways to live together. Ten minutes later, Coconut left the room and came back with her chewy, then went back to sleep. She knows the game.

Is it any different for us? We have to figure out where to draw the line, when to react, and when to be patient. The dogs seem to be interested in food, shelter, and companionship. They do what is necessary to keep those goals secure. Sometimes I think we would all do better if we remembered our real goals. We are so easily distracted into worrying about what we don't have or obsessed that we will lose what we do have, so things rather than goals become our focus.

If my goal is to love God and neighbor, or to allow faith to color my living, then momentary distractions, additions, or deletions to life aren't as dramatic as we sometimes make them. Tendencies to overreact out of selfishness or underreact out of fear might be replaced by remembering the big picture. We all live in a big house of faith, and God has provided the blessings of his presence and takes care of basic needs. I shouldn't have to watch my dogs to remember what that means and how it looks, but sometimes it helps when I do.

AN UNEXPECTED FATHER

✠ ✠ ✠

WHEN CAUGHT BY SURPRISE, OUR tendency is to react with anger or blame. How often do we go off like a firecracker whose fuse has already been lit? Such living is reactive rather than proactive. Think about the drama of a riot after a police shooting or a car bomb targeting an enemy. Reactive living is typically focused on anger and blame, whereas proactive living seeks to diffuse such drama before untreated hatred causes bigger problems.

Here is another scenario, more personal for me. When my uncle Bob died, my struggle was intensified by the fact that he had been my surrogate father the year my father served in Vietnam. In 1965, our parents moved us to Kansas City, near his family, in case Dad didn't come back from war. I was too young to understand this then, but my parents and Uncle Bob were being proactive with love. For a fourteen-year-old, this father figure was a gift! Uncle Bob and Aunt Barb were always full of love, faith, and joy. Bob always had a joke, and I can never remember him without a smile. We watched sports, played golf, he shared advice, and after babysitting my cousins (who were much younger), he and I would watch movies and snack before bedtime.

He didn't have to do that for me, but he did anyway. He loved Jesus.

He loved life. He loved his family. He loved my family. He celebrated life in every way he could. He only knew how to smile, and his love overpowered any temptation to be negative. That also made him a great pastor. Through his example, I am reminded to be a joyful example of Christ's love rather than letting the nonsense and pain of this world rule any living.

Because he and my parents were proactive, I had this great relationship (before anything happened), which continued to be a blessing beyond what anyone would have imagined. I suggest we would all do better to be Uncle Bob for someone else than be tempted to let reaction to sin poison our living. In that way, Christ will touch other lives, just as Uncle Bob's touched mine! What can be more proactive than that?

WHAT DOES JESUS LOOK LIKE?

✚ ✚ ✚

SO MANY PEOPLE HAVE PAINTED pictures of Jesus, but none were created during his time on earth. All came hundreds of years after his earthly life. And so many of them have the same look. You know what I mean—long brown hair, a trimmed beard, loving eyes, and a gentle face. What do you think Jesus looked like? Who really knows? And why is it even important?

One of my seminary professors had been a missionary in Japan immediately after World War II. He introduced me to the striking prints of a Japanese Christian artist named Sadao Watanabe. His prints depict Jesus, other biblical characters, and Bible stories using a traditional Japanese woodblock style of printing. Jesus and his disciples all look Japanese, with almond-shaped eyes and wearing kimonos. They are unusually different and immediately recognizable as his work. The stories are familiar, but the face of Jesus was not.

When I was in my first congregation, I had one such print on the wall behind my desk. This Watanabe print depicted Jesus and Mary. A woman came to my office, sat down, and during our conversation, she kept staring at that print. Finally, I asked her if she liked it. Her answer surprised me. She said, "No! That is so sacrilegious!" I was taken aback and asked why she had such strong feelings. Her response was "It doesn't look like Jesus," and she said that was offensive to her. After a momentary pause, I decided I needed to explain to her why I had that print on my wall.

I told her that none of us know what Jesus really looked like, but I agreed he did likely not look Japanese. I explained the reason I loved that print was it helped me to remember to look at Jesus through the eyes of someone else. It reminds me that we cannot capture Jesus with our own impressions but that he has captured the world with his love. No matter what color our skin or country of birth, everyone wants Jesus to look like them. The message of the Gospel is that Jesus wants us to look more like him, and that look is seen in washing feet, healing the sick, and befriending the outcasts.

More important than a picture of Jesus is what people see about Jesus in how you and I live. Watanabe reminds me of that and that Jesus is for an entire world, not just for me. She politely accepted my explanation and hopefully saw Jesus through new eyes.

NOVEMBER 22, 1963

✝ ✝ ✝

HERE IS WHAT I REMEMBER about November 22, 1963. I was an eighth grader living at West Point, New York, the location of the United States Military Academy, where my father was stationed at that time. It was the end of school day. We had grabbed books and jackets and were lined up waiting for the bell to ring. But something was off. My teacher said, "All after-school activities are cancelled," but didn't tell us why. Other teachers were in the hallway hugging and crying. The bell rang, and we started out.

At a time when no one cried in front of others, I was nervous and thought I'd say something clever. I blurted, "What's wrong? Did the president die?" From the look I got, I knew I had walked into a place I hadn't even imagined!

My teacher replied, "As a matter of fact, yes! He was assassinated!" Her eyes were full of tears as she added, "I wish you were as perceptive when it came to math!" I was so embarrassed and wished I could crawl under a rock.

In hindsight, at the time, I was probably shocked more by my callous remark than the death of a president. But that reality hit me too! Over time, I have learned how easily a quick comment can have unintended consequences. Thinking I was clever, I had hurt my teacher and embarrassed myself. Sometimes when we aren't sure what to say, we are often better off just keeping quiet. Words can never be taken back. If we aren't aware of someone else's situation, we often learn the hard way that some surprises are not worth walking into.

Servant love often involves simply being quiet and letting someone else lead us into their moment. Once we know what we are dealing with, we might know better what might be helpful (and what might not!). Listening is often a better and more helpful act of love than talking. My teacher could have made me feel it worse but let me down as gently as she could. From my mistake, I learned to listen. From her comment, I learned about forgiving love.

Those were pretty important lessons for me that day. And because I remember them today, I think they were good lessons. Love is often about listening before allowing our nervousness or pain to hurt someone else. Forgiveness works, and sometimes saying nothing is better than the wrong something!

HOME

✠ ✠ ✠

WHAT IS YOUR DEFINITION OF home? Is it a place or a state of mind? Is it a familiar building or is it wherever you are loved, nurtured, and feel safe? How many homes have you had, and is there one home that is more like home than any other?

As a child, I always had a place to live but never a place to call home. My dad was a career army officer, so we constantly relocated from one army post to another. We never lived anywhere long enough to put down roots, always being on the move. I always had a roof over my head and was embraced by loving parents and siblings. But every year or so, we lived in a different house, and there were never relatives or familiar memories and friends from years gone by. From kindergarten through high school, I went to twelve different schools. And yet we made each place we lived—whether Japan, Kansas, Missouri, Virginia, Maryland, Germany, New York, or anywhere else—feel like home. But none of those places were home for very long, and once they were behind us, someplace else had to do.

What place in your life is more a home than any other? I would like you to think for a while about the church. Your church! In a real sense, a congregation exists as a different kind of home but a home nonetheless.

This is a place where family events take place—baptisms, funerals, confirmation, weddings, and the like. It is a place where we gather for nourishment and support. It is a family we are not genetically related to; instead, we are related through the blood of Christ. We worship and pray. We laugh and cry. We support mutual ministries and welcome visitors looking for stability and peace into our midst. This is a constant in our lives, always ready to welcome and always full of the love, life, energy, and purpose we associate with *home*.

As we traveled from place to place, I realize now why it was so important for my parents to always find a place to worship. That always helped wherever we lived to feel more like home. This is one of God's gifts of grace that blesses us with the potential of being a spiritual home in a world that often feels lonely, selfish, and distant. In a sense, it is our home away from home during our journeys on earth, until that day when we reach our real and eternal home!

JOE FROM IRELAND

✚ ✚ ✚

ROXANNE AND I HAD NEVER traveled outside of the country, even though we love to experience new places and scenery. One year, we decided to take a trip overseas, and Ireland, for a variety of reasons, was our choice. And a great one it was! Ireland's scenery was beautiful. The little villages, the history, the charm of local pubs, and the history were all incredible. But the warmth of people we met was even more so.

There was an older man named Joe we will never forget. He volunteered in a little museum in Straide that was attached to an old abbey. He asked if we had family that had come from this little village, as tourists only showed up there if they were related somehow. We told him we didn't have any family from Ireland. He was amazed! He said no one from America came to that little village unless they were searching their roots. He couldn't believe that we wanted to see the real Ireland and not just the big cities. He called us over and over again "proper Americans," as if it were a badge of honor for us!

We spent about an hour in conversation, and he then told us about a dream trip he had taken to the United States. He said he had always had a bucket list for if he went to America, and he told us what was on that list. His goals had been to visit Los Angeles, a Pacific beach, a

Las Vegas casino, and the Hoover Dam and ride on a Greyhound bus. A Greyhound bus? Now that caught us off guard! We were living the dream by going to Ireland, and he had done the same by a bus ride in the US! He wondered why we, with no Irish roots, were interested in Ireland, and we wondered why a Greyhound bus could seem so attractive. But more important was our conversation and how that never would have occurred if we had been too busy to stop and visit. How much we miss when we are too busy to slow down and listen!

I wonder how many Joes I walk by every day, without stopping to find out what is important to him or her. What is missed when I don't give someone else the chance to ask the same of me? How often have I done the same with Roxanne, my children, or any people I am around—all because I was too busy or preoccupied to listen, to ask questions, to share? Why was Joe so important? Why not? When we slow down and take time to listen, we discover that many little things in life are more important than the big things we can't get off our minds. When we take time to listen, we find out how much we can find in common and how simple things can mean so much.

Why did I have to go all the way to Ireland to remember why it is important to slow down and listen? More important is whether I will remember a lesson learned! Why do I let myself get so busy that I forget it is in the simple acts of love that life is really filled? Being quiet, paying attention, asking rather than assuming, and listening doesn't cost anything other than time. And what time is better spent than that? And isn't this just another way of washing feet? If God can take time to listen to me, well, you know what comes next!

STOREFRONTS AT NIGHT

✛ ✛ ✛

WHEN I STARTED TAKING PHOTOGRAPHY classes, I began to look for new ideas and new places to shoot photos. I wanted to be creative and see things that I often missed. One thing I started doing was driving downtown late at night and looking at the lighted storefront windows, which are so much more powerful than in daylight! In the darkness of the night, it doesn't take much light to make a difference. There is so much we miss during the brightness and busyness of the day that is clarified in the darkness of the night.

When the only light in a store is a spotlight in the display window, objects come to life and colors shout out to be noticed. There is a bridal gown shop in downtown Kalamazoo that I have photographed often at night. Without daytime distractions and surrounded by darkness of winter's night, any glimpse of color is much more intense than we normally would notice. How amazing that in the darkest night, some things are more visible than in the light of day!

With such a fact clear, you now understand the goal of the season in the church year we call Epiphany, which means to reveal or make something known. How did wise men from a distant land find the infant Jesus, except by a solitary light in the darkness of the sky? That is why we string lights on houses during this dark season of winter. There is a light that is brighter than any darkness, and that light is our infant Savior and his love. In the midst of winter's darkest hour, we celebrate the true light! With Christmas behind, it is time to carry the joy of Jesus's birth into the world's darkness.

Rather than being depressed by the shadows of sin, allow your faith, smiles, and servant love to become a torch that brightens the world in which you live. Faith is not only your strength but a beacon others will notice and a flare that changes the way people react to shadows in their own lives. Window dressers know what they are doing when they leave a spotlight on valuable commodities (even when stores are closed).

God calls us to let the light shine because there are always many who are still wandering in shadows and darkness, waiting for someone, somehow, to share a glimpse of hope. Remember, in the darkness of night, it doesn't take much light to make a difference! And so a baby was born late at night in a little village, with only the glow of candlelight for a reason! May the joy of the Christ child be the sparkle and glow of your Christmas! Let that brilliant love fill your eyes, your smiles, and your warm embraces with the gift of true light!

CRACKER JACKS

✠ ✠ ✠

THIS WILL DATE ME, BUT many might still be able to relate with their own experiences with the quintessential American treat: Cracker Jacks! And I am not talking about today's cheap imitation but the good old days when there were real prizes (plastic animals, toys, mini books, rings, or a little magnifying glass). Today's prizes pale in comparison to those of old. In fact, I am not even sure if there is a prize inside anymore! But that is not the point.

My parents thought a box of Cracker Jacks for my brother and me to share was a great treat. They didn't have much spending money, and all that caramel corn for a few cents was a bargain. They meant well but didn't understand Don and I didn't care about the popcorn; we just wanted the prize! There was only one, so we each had different tricks as we got close to the bottom of the box to make sure we were the one who got the prize.

As we were supposed to love each other, we had to act very innocent when one of acted surprised and said, "Oh, look! I got the prize! Sorry!" As I think about my brotherly struggles with one of us winning and one losing, I can't help but think about St. Paul's response to his own impending death. While the world sees death as a loss, Paul saw it as the moment of opening the gift of eternal life. No matter what strategies we attempt, there is no way to escape death, yet as Paul faced that reality, he was filled with joy. For he knew there was already a prize waiting for him, and he would get in no matter what. That was more powerful than the thought of losing his life.

More powerful yet is that Paul shared many such thoughts while imprisoned in Rome. He was literally inside a box from which there was no escape, yet he didn't feel alone. Paul reminds us that in the empty box called death, there is a prize called Easter that is already our gift. Pilate thought Jesus was trapped in a tomb, yet he was the prize waiting to be revealed for all time! By faith, we already have that gift in hand. It is more permanent and valuable than any Cracker Jack prize, and no earthly strategy is needed. It is not a cheap imitation of better gifts from other times. It is a gift! It is ours! And it is free! How could there be a better prize than that?

SIGNS FROM GOD

✝ ✝ ✝

DON'T YOU WISH GOD WOULD talk to us like he did with people long ago? You know what I mean, don't you? Isaiah heard God. So did Abraham and Isaac and Jacob. Joseph had dreams. Moses was given a sign on Sinai. John the Baptist was clear in what he was to say. St. Paul had that blinding light vision. And the list goes on and on. Whether dreams, or parables, or a distinct voice, others heard God. But does that happen today?

Is God silent, or is it possible we maybe aren't listening? Years ago, I was afraid for my first wife as she faced an incredibly difficult surgery. We didn't know the outcome and were fearful that she was going to die. I prayed and cried and begged for a sign or some sort of help with my fears. I didn't know what to expect but was at the end of my rope. Sitting in my office, I just stared out at the parking lot at church, because I couldn't concentrate on anything. And right in front of my window was a deer.

It was facing me. I turned away and tried to get busy myself with work to get my mind off the surgery. Then I stopped and looked again. The deer was still there. It hadn't moved. I had never seen a deer in the church parking lot before. As I looked, I had a remarkable and unexplainable feeling of peace. I knew the surgery would be successful. I don't know how, but I had peace. But there is more!

Now I look often for that deer and have seen many others, all the time. On that day, the first day I saw a deer, it seemed such a powerful answer to prayer. But now I realize the deer are always wandering through the lot. My problem long ago was that I was so busy and preoccupied with my work and busyness that I missed what is so obvious today. I was likely surrounded by signs and messages from God daily, but I was too busy with me to let God break through. What I have learned is that God speaks daily in a variety of ways. And all it takes to hear and see is to take my eyes off of me and be aware. After all, that is the essence of prayer. We need to listen to hear God knocking at the door. And we have to open our eyes to see his signs! The surrender of faith opens the door, opens our eyes, and always fills our hearts with the miracle of peace!

THAT HEALING TOUCH

✚ ✚ ✚

ONE DAY, JESUS RUSHED TO keep a young girl from dying. Along the way, he was delayed as a woman pushed through the crowd to seek healing for her own disease. Amazingly, just by touching his robe, she was healed. According to the Gospel accounts, Jesus asked who had touched him and commented about feeling power leave him. The story is pretty unique in the Gospels, as a woman simply touched Jesus's robe, and a surge of healing changed her life! I have always wondered about that scene but now see it in a new light.

Four years after cancer surgery, my blood work continued to be good. The cancer was gone. And then in my next visit, the doctor said, "The results of your blood work lead me to believe there might still be some cells growing at the site of the surgery." I was stunned. I couldn't breathe. My doctor said radiation was necessary to kill off remaining cancer cells. I was afraid and wondered if I would ever be healed. Would this bring death sooner than later? I was afraid. He scheduled the radiation, and I'll never forget that first treatment.

As I lay in the tube for the first time, I was shaking and afraid. But then, for some reason, as I was praying for calm and peace, I remembered the story of the woman who was healed by the touch of

Jesus's robe. As I was being touched by radiation, an invisible force of energy, I thought of that miracle. It came to mind that radiation is the source of creation itself. A gift of God!

Radiation is part of everything, unleashing the incredible power of destruction and even the gift of healing. I thought about the big bang (science's way of saying God is the explosive energy of creation) and remembered how a woman was healed when power flowed out of Jesus's body. When that woman was healed by touching his robe, Jesus mentioned he felt a discharge of energy. I wondered if that was like a machine bombarding me with radiation. And that image became my meditative prayer.

As I lay in that machine listening to the whooshing and whirring sounds, I thought about what the woman must have heard as Jesus scurried by. The wind in his robes and whoosh of his shuffling sandals were the sounds just before she was touched by Jesus's healing power! Suddenly in a noisy radiation machine, this cold, empty tomb of a tube felt safe, and I felt peace! From then on, every time I went into that tube, and each time the whirring and whooshing of the machine started, I remembered that woman, the sound of Jesus rushing by, the energy discharge from Jesus, and the gift of faith that Jesus said was the power of this woman's healing.

That became the visualization of my prayer in every treatment. a powerful comfort and the assurance of healing peace. That was many years ago, but I remember it as if it were yesterday. Such moments are why Bible stories are indeed Living Words. And such a simple story became my powerful prayer!

A FEDEX ENCOUNTER

✠ ✠ ✠

MY WIFE'S LAW OFFICE WAS in downtown Kalamazoo. One day, she got a phone call from a woman on the north side of town—literally the other side of the tracks, as Amtrak runs through the middle of downtown. She explained she had a FedEx package with Roxanne's name on it. Rox wasn't expecting a package and wasn't sure what to think but said she would drive over to the woman's house to see what the package was. But her schedule was so hectic she couldn't leave the office, so I offered to go rather than making that kind woman wait.

I pulled up to her house, walked onto her porch, and rang the doorbell. I was greeted by a smiling woman who had the package. She told me that she had received three parcels but only expected two. Then she checked the name on the third and realized it wasn't a package for her. She googled Roxanne's name until she found a business address and then tracked her down by phone. In this day and age, for someone to go out of their way for someone they don't know is remarkable! She could have just as easily called FedEx and had them pick up the box. But she didn't, which took special care and concern, so there was no way I was going to just take the box and run.

As I introduced myself, I handed her my business card so she knew I was who I said I was. And we continued in a very personal and pleasant conversation. We talked about her church, and then she asked if I, by any chance, knew anyone who had a house for rent. She said the landlord wouldn't fix the many problems in her house and kept raising the rent. I told her I didn't know of anything off hand but would check around. Her parting words were the best. She said, "I thought to ask, because even though this seems just a chance encounter, I believe God always has a purpose when he brings people together." Amen!

Such a powerful faith is refreshing! And I was reminded that when I take time to actually talk to a stranger (or anyone) in more than just a causal and off-handed way, I always learn more than I was expecting. I was blessed by her confident faith. Had it not been for FedEx delivering to a wrong address, we never would have met. Whether God's plan was for this to help her find a place to rent or just for two strangers to have a conversation, I'll never know. But God was certainly present! And I am so glad that I remembered to take the time to listen to someone I was a stranger to.

WHO IS JESUS?

✠ ✠ ✠

EVERY YEAR, BY THE END of summer, high school graduates have either settled into a job or begun to continue education in college as they move into the world of being an adult. Suddenly, life becomes more real, and decisions more personal. Things that were easy to ignore just a few months ago become more relevant. I remember one September when a young man from our church had just stared college and emailed me with a request for a class he was taking. He was writing a paper for a religion class and was to ask his home pastor some questions. He asked me, "Who do you think Jesus really was?"

There were other specific questions, such as "What did Jesus stand for?" and "How do you differentiate the Jesus of history and the Christ of faith?" Those were important questions, and I understood quickly he didn't want standard answers with fancy theological terms but personal views in my own words, as if he and I were just having a normal conversation. In other words, he was asking for me to share my faith in words he could understand.

My first thought was *Don't you know what I believe?* And then I realized that wasn't his question. Many pastors believe different things about Jesus, and in this class, there would be a lot of different answers to the same question. Some might be wrong, some might be right, but certainly all would be different. He wasn't looking for what Luther, or Matthew, or St. Paul said about Jesus. His assignment was to know what I would say and how I would say it. And so I wrote out what I thought would be helpful to him but also understandable to whoever else might read my words. I took an hour and wrote down some words that I hoped would be helpful in his paper. At the same time, I thought, *This really is a great exercise for me!*

Most would assume I know all those answers, but it isn't often that I have to sit down and be that specific for an out-of-the-blue request. No one had asked me such questions in a long time, maybe never. I really had to stop and think about how I would put into my words what I believe. I don't know what kind of grade he got on his paper, but I know how much that exercise helped me to grow!

And now, here is what I ask you: Who do *you* believe Jesus is? And before you give a stock answer, let me beg you to think about how you would say it in your words, not quoting a Bible text or the catechism or anyone else. Who is Jesus to you and for you? Take some time and think about it, and maybe you'll be more ready than I was when, out of the blue, someone asks, "Who is Jesus?"

WHOSE BIRTHDAY IS IT?

✛ ✛ ✛

WHEN OUR PARENTS HAVE A birthday, we always give them a gift, send a card, or call on the phone. Right? On our birthdays, they do the same for us. I recently had a personal revelation that will change how I approach my mom on my next birthday. Here is what happened. My birthday is only a week before Mom's. I gave her our gift a few days before her birthday, as I was in town for a visit. On her birthday, I forgot to call, but I did so the day after. When she answered, I said, "Hi, Mom. Happy birthday!"

She said, "Thanks, but you already gave me a gift!"

Then I stumbled into something that hit me like a flash in the dark. And so I tried it out on her. "Mom," I said, "I just realized that I really should have called you on *my* birthday!" I was feeling surprisingly inspired. I continued, "Mom, I think we do birthdays all wrong. I shouldn't just call you on your birthday; I should call you on mine!"

She said, "I don't understand."

I told her, "I receive a gift from you on my birthday, but I had nothing to do with being born. If it weren't for you and Dad, I wouldn't have a birthday at all. You should get birthday gifts from me, and I should be calling you on my birthday and saying, 'Thanks for birthing me!'" She laughed. (Well, more appropriately for my mom is that she giggled.) We talked some more and said good bye.

This week, she called me about something else and then said, "Tim, I was thinking about what you said about your birthday, that you should be calling me and Dad on that day. I want you to know I have been thinking about that because it meant a lot to me." Now, I share this not to prove anything other than sometimes a blind squirrel can find a nut and to confess how often it is easy for me to miss what is obvious, especially for those who have done so much for me! I will definitely celebrate my birthday differently from now on. It is just a thought, but I felt it might be worth sharing.

THE EASY WAY ISN'T
ALWAYS THE BEST WAY

✠ ✠ ✠

ONE DAY IN TOLEDO, I was taking Communion to a widow confined to her home. She was always unpleasant, grumpy, and very hard of hearing. She was not an easy visit. As I drove to her house, I wondered if I could come up with an excuse to go somewhere else. But I had promised I would come, and so I knew I had to. Guilt and obligation are tough words but often work their magic. As I stepped on to her porch and started to ring her doorbell, I noticed the strong odor of gas. Was I imagining it? No! I backed away, but there was no odor outside except by the front door. It was coming from inside!

My heart started raced, and I wondered what to do. I went again to ring the doorbell but stopped. Would that cause an explosion? I didn't know. It was before cell phones, and there wasn't time to go door-to-door, asking someone to call for help. I slowly opened the door and called out, "Wilma! Are you there?" She was and asked me to come in. The smell of gas in her house was overpowering. She was sitting on the couch, complaining about a terrible headache. I had her stand up and slowly walked her outside. I left the door open and went into the kitchen where a burner on her gas stove was on but not lit. I turned it off, slowly opened every window, and sat outside with Wilma on her porch. After about fifteen minutes, the odor was gone.

Knowing we were safe, and with her headache gone, we went in, and I gave her Communion. Everything was OK. When I left, I sat in my car, and the realization of what could have been overpowered me. I started trembling. And then I prayed. What if I hadn't gone? What if I had delayed? What if I hadn't noticed the gas and pushed the doorbell? Why did this happen today?

To this day, I am convinced it was not a coincidence that I was there when I was there. And the selfishness I felt for not wanting to be there was tempered with the reality that if I had taken the easy way out, something tragic might have happened. There are so many times we are reminded that the easy way is not always the best way, and sometimes God has plans for us that we would never guess. We never know when we are the angel God is sending to someone else. And yet, come to think of it, we do know, don't we?

MY SISTER STOPPED
FOR A STRANGER

✛ ✛ ✛

MY SISTER IS A NURSE. One day, she and her husband were driving to their home in rural Virginia and witnessed a horrendous accident right in front of them on the interstate. A truck pulled into a lane too quickly and clipped a motorcycle. The driver of the bike was thrown onto the side of the road. Her husband quickly shouted, "We need to stop!" and grabbed the cell phone to dial 911. My sister ran from the car and began to administer CPR for the victim, until paramedics arrived.

She told me later that she heard on the radio the young man died on the way to the hospital. She was quite naturally affected and felt badly she couldn't help save his life. She hoped the man had known he wasn't alone and someone had tried to help. She later posted these thoughts for her friends to read:

> Today I met a man. I loved him and I briefly coaxed his broken body into considering life over death. But it was not meant to be. For a moment I comforted him, embraced him as if he were my own family. Tonight I am saddened by the news of his death. I am a nurse,

far removed from practice, yet always a nurse. I hope the greatest gift I gave today was a caring, loving spirit to transition his spirit to a better place. Thank you, all my nursing friends and first responders! I am reminded why I chose the profession I did many years ago. Peace to the family of this stranger I loved!

I know it was more than nursing training that guided her reaction; it was the training of her parents (whom I know quite well) who taught her what it means to live like Jesus. Such love of God and neighbor filters into her nursing and being a mom, a wife, and a friend. This is what discipleship looks like. It is more than memorizing Bible passages or showing up each week for worship. It is becoming so comfortable in our skin of faith that the love of God changes how we live every moment of our lives. Anyone can show up in worship, but being a disciple means our desire to love God and neighbor is so ingrained it just happens. This is what our children need to learn, and this is what we need to help one another remember. Jesus's goal for his disciples is that we might be so changed by his love that we begin to daily look and act more and more like him. In a world filled with much anger and loneliness, this is the light that can be so helpful in keeping people from dying alone.

A JEEP IN THE BLIZZARD

✠ ✠ ✠

MY GOOD FRIEND FRED SHARED this personal story, and I will try to do justice to it. Fred taught at Western Michigan University and was the faculty representative to the NCAA. It was late March. He was on the Ohio turnpike, headed to Cleveland for the conference basketball tournament. As so often happens in northwest Ohio, there was a late winter storm that blew in off the lake. The road was slippery. Visibility was terrible. Fred said he was straining to see and wasn't aware yet of a terrible accident occurring just ahead of him.

He said he suddenly saw nothing but red taillights of cars and semis at a standstill. Visibility was zero. He was trying to slow down and stop, but in his rearview mirror, he saw lights coming at full speed toward him. He wasn't sure what to do and knew he would be hit. A car in the lane to his left was stopped as well. There was nowhere to go! Fred said he didn't even see it coming, but suddenly there was a jeep passing on the right shoulder. He motioned for Fred to follow.

As he started to pull over to follow the jeep around stalled traffic, he glanced to his left. The guy in the left lane had a hollow look, and he and Fred made eye contact just as Fred pulled away. As he got out of that lane, he heard the noise of traffic emerging from the blizzard and crashing into both lanes of traffic. Ultimately, fifty vehicles were involved, and the man who had his gaze fixed on Fred was one who was killed.

Fred followed the jeep, pulling back on the road in front of traffic still stopped by the accident. He said there were two things he could never get over. First was the look in the eye of the driver next to him, realizing what was coming next. The other was that as Fred pulled back on the road, the jeep he was following suddenly wasn't there anymore. It just wasn't there, and he was alone!

He drove down the highway all alone and always wondered where that jeep went—or if it had really been there at all! He spoke of that often and wondered about what had happened. Was it the hand of God? The touch of an angel? Moments such as that are full of questions and no easy answers, but Fred always felt God had touched him for a reason. He didn't understand all that had happened, but its impact never left. We all wrestle in the same way with such moments. We wonder. We make assumptions. Ultimately, faith is the only answer we can cling to. Fred was OK with the questions, because he also was OK with faith as his answer.

THE CANDY LADY

✠ ✠ ✠

CHRISTMAS PREPARATIONS INVOLVE BAKING COOKIES. One December, I was dispatched by Roxanne to find a particular candy she needed for the topping on her cookies. And those little chocolates would surely be found at a small business called the Candy Lady.

I arrived at the shop and went in to find a cheerful grandma behind the register who knew exactly what I was looking for. I bought what was needed, and as I was getting out some cash, a little girl came out from the back room and stood behind the register. I asked who she might be. The candy lady beamed and said, "My granddaughter." I gave her cash for the candy, and her grandma showed her how to put it in the register and then had her count out and hand me the change. It was such a special moment to see such a bond of love! As the little girl put the change in my hand, I said, "Thank you." It was obvious she enjoyed helping.

As it was only a week before Christmas, and since we were in the midst of all our preparations, I was really in the Christmas mood and had a moment of inspiration. I took the two dollars that were my change and asked the candy lady if I could give it to her granddaughter as a tip. She smiled and told me it was OK. So I told the little girl that her grandma must be so proud of how much help she was and what a great job she was doing. I told her this was just for her—a thank you for being so helpful.

The smile I got in return from that little girl was more priceless than anything I had seen all day. And it was infectious. It just added to the joy of the pre-Christmas spirit and made me feel more special than I had when I walked in. I was struck by how little it took to make another person smile—and all because I was in the mood for Christmas. But I wonder, why can't I share that same joy every day? If Christmas has brought such joy to my life, why not live every day with that same love and joy? There is no reason I can't! All it takes is remembering. And you can too. Why wait until a week before Christmas? Isn't every day a time to prepare for Jesus to come into every life? And we can help!

CATHEDRALS

✠ ✠ ✠

MY WIFE AND I HAVE had the privilege of several trips to Europe. I am drawn to the massive cathedrals and marvel at their construction and craftsmanship and how they have stood for so long. These massive structures would be too expensive and impractical to build today, and finding craftsmen who could even do the work would likely be impossible. Like all the other tourists, we marveled at the beauty of the cathedrals with their stained glass, marble carvings, pipe organs, and massive carved doors of wood or bronze.

Some criticize these magnificent creations in which no one worships anymore and question whether there was ever any value in all of the art that made these centers of worship and community life so special. In every cathedral, we listened to the tour guides explain the biblical meanings of the art and how important it was in an age where most people were illiterate. As I reflect, I have gained an even greater appreciation for such gifts. Such art told the biblical story. It created an atmosphere. Inspired by God, this art beckoned people to feel close to God.

But until now, I never thought about our own age of biblical illiteracy, where such art is seen as outdated and stiff. And yet thousands pass through these cathedrals daily. Millions each year. And they hear the story! Every visitor (whether biblically literate or not, whether Christian or atheist) hears about the biblical stories depicted by long-dead craftsmen. Hundreds and hundreds of years after statues, columns, arches, carved doors, and stained glass were created, they continue to proclaim Christ!

What artist or craftsman ever imagined their work would touch lives from every corner of the world? And beyond worshipping communities, the tourists who crowd into these buildings (whether they realize it or not) are being told the stories of Christmas and Easter and the miracle of a heavenly home. Who would believe that cold stone or cut glass could have such life? Does it make a difference? Who is to say?

But here is my real question: What are we leaving behind for those who come after our earthly journey is over? What have we created by how we love, how we serve, how we teach, and how we give that will last behind our last earthly breath? This is not to encourage guilt but rather to inspire daily creative and loving service. The church should be all about daily creating living art. We can't all be Michelangelo, or Bach, or Luther, but we have opportunities to use our gifts to touch the world around us with the love of Jesus. It doesn't matter if we know who it will touch. Just know that it will!

OPUS AND ATTICUS

✠ ✠ ✠

ONE OF MY FAVORITE CARTOON strips was *Bloom County*. It was unique and edgy. It was creative. It made me laugh. I have learned that its creator, Berkeley Breathed, modeled *Bloom County* after the southern hometown of Harper Lee, the author of *To Kill a Mockingbird*. Breathed's childhood hero was Atticus Finch, a soft-spoken white attorney who defended a black man in the segregated South. The recent publication of an earlier draft of that novel, *Go Set a Watchman*, presented Finch in older years as a typically prejudiced old man. And for many, an image was destroyed.

I read that Breathed was bothered by the new image of Atticus Finch, which caused him to remember a fan letter from Harper Lee many years past. Apparently, she had begged him *not* to ever cease *Bloom County*, as the character of Opus (the penguin) had been so important for her. The irony of the situation confused him, as he was devastated by the release of *Go Set a Watchman*, which upset his image of Atticus Finch as a beacon of equality in the prejudiced South.

The reality of Harper Lee begging him not to surrender such an important character by ending a comic strip, while a later novel attributed to her destroyed his image of Atticus Finch, is quite an irony.

She had asked him not to do to her what, in essence, had been done to him with the release of this novel. He was frustrated with losing his childhood image of Atticus Finch, just as she was frustrated when he stopped *Bloom County* and she lost her favored Opus. What a wonderful illustration of the world in which we live.

We would like everything to be the way we want and struggle when idols are revealed to have clay feet. We anguish as others do what we have done ourselves. It is confusing. What we want and what we do are often at odds, and what we like to receive is not always what we are willing to share. Both Breathed and Lee were creating fiction, yet fiction is a way of sharing reality without readers realizing they are being invited to look into a mirror. The good news is that forgiveness and grace are not fiction and have power to overcome what we do to ourselves and others. And that story will continue to be written and shared and lived forever. That finally restores real peace.

POLICE RIDE ALONG

✠ ✠ ✠

AT VARIOUS TIMES, I HAVE ridden with police officers on patrol, wanting to learn more about what they face. One of the members of our congregation was a cop, and I also wanted to do this to be supportive of her. I wanted to witness firsthand some of the moments in the daily life of a city that I am often insulated from. Several years ago, on such a night, the officer I was with was sent to an apartment where two unmarried parents were fighting over custody of a two-year-old boy.

The dad had been raising his son, and the birth mom had shown up at midnight and demanded to take the boy away. The dad was working as a janitor. He lived in an apartment that was sparse but clean. The mom was dressed in a smock that a hairdresser might wear and was screaming at the police and the father of her child. There were already four officers in the apartment when we got there, and I stayed in the hallway. I noticed a little girl, about five, with braided hair accentuated by beads.

She look tired and scared and was standing all alone. I knelt down and told her she had beautiful hair. Suddenly her face lit up, and I saw a sparkle in her eyes that had not been there before. I saw life.

Overhearing the conversation from the apartment, I learned the mom had five children from five different fathers. She took care of two girls, and the other three were raised by their fathers. Each month, she would go and take those other children home for one day so they were all with her when the social worker made her monthly visit. The mom was making certain she got all the welfare money for each child, even though she was not raising them herself. This father had petitioned the court for custody, and his hearing was the next day. It was a terrible standoff, and all I could think was that the sparkle I saw in that little girl's eyes was a bright light her mom was slowly chasing away. It was depressing to know ahead of time the struggles this little girl would face.

At the same time, it was awesome to see a man working so hard to give his child a stable and loving life. It was a tale of two cities I will never forget. And it reminded me how important it is for all of us to do what we can to keep sparkling eyes from growing dim. We can't change all the realities of a broken world, but understanding how difficult life is and doing what we can to bring smiles into life is certainly a place to start.

DO ANGELS PUSH CARS?

✚ ✚ ✚

RECENTLY, MY CAR DIED. WHAT I mean is one minute it was doing what a car should do, and suddenly it just stopped, and every warning light on the dashboard lit up. It was like monitors in a hospital room that all start beeping and flashing at the same time. This fairly new, well-maintained, great-looking car (certainly an extension of my personality) was no longer a functioning car. The engine simply self-destructed! But here is what is amazing.

We were traveling at 70 mph on a local four-lane highway, about half a mile south of our exit, when the warning lights went on and the car got quiet. I pushed the accelerator, but nothing happened. The engine stopped. I quickly shifted into neutral and tried the key. Nothing! The engine was dead, but we were coasting and still at least a quarter mile from the exit. Luckily, we still had some speed heading toward the ramp.

Questions filled my head. Would I make it to the ramp? Up the ramp? What if there was traffic at the intersection? Amazingly, we rolled up the ramp, through the stop sign, past a green light, and turned toward a gas station. I had no power for steering or brakes (just like the good old days), and as the car was about to stop, I jumped out and pushed and steered into a parking space at the nearby gas station. We were stopped!

For me, this was incredible! It would be easy to scream about a lost car. Anger is normal when things don't go as we wish or events we don't deserve surprise us. We grumble. We complain. We can feel sorry for ourselves. We can even blame God. But how in the world did the engine blow up when it did, rather than twenty minutes earlier when we were ten miles out in the middle of farm roads? And how did we coast as far as we did, get up a ramp, through an intersection, and into a parking space?

Incredibly, for someone likes me who wants answers and likes to be in control, I found myself sitting in a dead car thinking more about how we made it to a safe place than losing an engine. So, does God handle dying cars? Was it all coincidence? Do guardian angels push? I do not know. But I do know that I am more amazed by how we got to safety than by how a car that was in great shape suddenly wasn't! Things don't always go our way, but sometimes we forget things can go differently than they should. I think I'm better off giving God credit for safety rather than cursing my loss! What do you think?

POKÉMON AND ZOMBIES

✚ ✚ ✚

THE IMAGE OF LIFELESS BODIES with glazed looks walking en masse toward a victim is more than I can handle. (Which is why I never understood the fascination of zombie movies.) How about you? Several years ago, the Pokémon Go app on people's cell phones brought this image to a neighborhood near you! It was as if a hidden population suddenly surfaced from out of the mist!

Apparently there were two locations on our church property where people were sent to capture their own pocket monsters. (I still don't understand the concept.) For weeks, our parking lot was besieged by young adults slowly walking around in circles, staring at cell phone screens for guidance.

Downtown, the scene was similar: people walking silently, staring with a blank gaze at screens. At night, the city park downtown looked like the set of a horror movie with packs of bodies moving quietly through the dark. I am surprised more were not hit by cars or injured by walking into trees! They did look like zombies—bodies moving with no expression, no noise, just a glazed stare as if being pulled by an unseen force.

Some have rationalized that this app brought people together.

(*Yeah*, I thought, *like zombies!*) At the same time, think about how many people you know who live with that same look as they move through life, pulled by unseen forces, unaware of where they are headed, hoping that at the end of their journey there will be a prize? How much time is wasted staring at screens, just going through the motions, or sleepwalking through life without any sense of joy or passion? Or without any inclination to engage with or serve others and celebrate Christ through faithful living? How many shuffle in a solitary walk and miss the beauty that is so near or the daily opportunities to make a difference in other lives? How many walking dead surround us?

Jesus calls us out of that lifeless walk, gives purpose and joy to the journey, and invites us to share with others the good news that the prize at the end of our journey is already in our hands. Part of our mission as a Christ's people is to reach out with the good news that the search is over. Another part of our mission is to be understanding of the needs of others and be ready to offer support to anyone who is looking for help. How can you help bring life to those still searching?

A LABOR OF LOVE

✠ ✠ ✠

ONE YEAR, WE VISITED MY son, Chris, a week before Labor Day. They were living in a suburb of Chicago, while I was living in Kalamazoo, Michigan. He, grandson Jack, and I went to a museum full of old steam engines, locomotives, and passengers cars from the golden age of railroading. After our visit, I said goodbye and began my journey home. While I was driving, Chris called and asked if my sermon for Sunday was done yet. I told him I had one but would need to read it again and make sure I still wanted to preach it. He said, "I'll write one for you." We laughed, and I kept driving. When I got home a few hours later, I checked my email, and he had indeed written a sermon.

He began by saying Labor Day was created in 1894 to celebrate the hard work of railroad workers following a bloody railroad strike, in which many died at the hands of the military and US marshals. He commented that he felt it fitting that he and I had just visited a museum in which we could see firsthand the result of (as Chris said) the "blood, sweat, and tears" of workers more than a hundred years ago. He concluded his sermon by saying the sacrifice of lives to build the trains, lay the tracks, and suffer during the conflict of a great train strike could be a Labor Day reminder of a greater labor of sacrifice by

Jesus Christ for you and me—a God who served rather than demanded service!

What moved me most in Chris's sermon was his emphasis on God's sacrifice of love for you and me. And his application that our labor as Christians is to wash feet, prepare the table, and invite guests. He is right. Labor Day is a national holiday, but for Christians, our labor is always about loving service, and we celebrate that gift and make every day holy by serving!

I rewrote my sermon that night, as it made sense to first comment about what Chris had done, which was to sit down and do something special for me. Labor Day is behind us, yet God's sacrifice of love for us makes every day God's labor day. I did use some of Chris's comments in my sermon, but more importantly, I was touched by his love and going out of his way to let me know that his faith was important, and his love for his father was important too. That labor of love was a reminder of how easily any of us can let others know that we get it.

GETTING SKUNKED

✚ ✚ ✚

ONE SUMMER, OUR SHAGGY, LOVELY dog named Coconut got skunked. It was a first for all of us and became one of those things that didn't just go away. Luckily, we confined her right away to the laundry room, but the whole house was tainted by her bad choice of what to stick her nose into. It was a long, dark, pungent night for all of us (and probably even longer for her). We washed her a couple times, aired out the house, and threw all of the towels outside. However, the journey had just begun. The next day, we found out the right solution to wash her with and gave her more baths. We threw away all of the soiled towels, and the odor that only a momma skunk can appreciate slowly began to dissipate. (Please notice I said *slowly*!)

All of you who have had similar adventures know that some aromas linger more than others. And even after six weeks, we would occasionally get a whiff of that terrible night. I share this not to elicit sympathy but as a reminder of the powerful aroma of sinful actions and a broken world. Bad stuff doesn't just leave a foul odor for a single night but can linger for days or even a lifetime. Sin is the smelly scent of Satan, and sometimes through no fault of our own, we get skunked by sin. (And sometimes it is our fault.) But in either case, the result is the same, and we all know the pain and terrible memories that ensue. Our actions cannot remove the scent of sin.

Apologies and appropriate reparations can help. Learning from our mistakes can often keep us from repeating offenses, but that stink can linger. How embarrassing is it for any of us when others can tell when we walk in the room what has happened? On the other hand, there is a solution that can not only erase the stain of sin but also set us free to start all over, as if we had never been skunked in the first place. Forgiveness lets us start over, and grace means that the sweet aroma of an empty tomb and a God of love can become the perfume of our living and the gift we can share with others who need help dealing with the realities of a sinful world and darky, skunky nights!

WHEN YOUR WATCH
STOPS WORKING

✠ ✠ ✠

I LOVED MY WATCH. IT was a special gift and easy to take for granted, until the batteries died. The only problem then was finding someone with the right tools to take it apart without scratching the cover or breaking the waterproof seal. Finally it was fixed. But a month later, the stem broke, and it would have cost more to fix it than buy a new watch. So Roxanne came through for me and found a new watch, just like my old one. And there was a new feature. It didn't use a battery at all but was solar powered. No need to ever open the cover or replace a battery. Perfect!

At least that was what I thought—until the first week in December when I noticed it was a half hour off. Upon closer inspection, I realized it had stopped. That couldn't be! It was still fairly new. As I slid my cuff back down over the watch, I realized what had happened. It was winter in Michigan, meaning long-sleeve shirts and no sunshine. I rolled my sleeve up, held the watch under my desk light, and it starting working right away. It has been fine since.

So, solar power is a problem in western Michigan's winters, where clouds are the norm. Hiding the watch under my shirt cuffs added to the problem. My watch needed more time in the light. In many ways, it is no different from us.

No matter how strong our faith and positive our outlook on life, when we are surrounded by too many clouds, negativity, and gloom, we are similarly affected. We aren't solar powered, but the energy and source of our living is often called the Light of the World! When we don't take time for prayer, worship, forgiving, and serving love in our own lives, we react as my watch did. The light of Jesus's love is the power of faith and hope-filled living. Without that energy source, we are as useless as a watch that can't keep time. Find time to soak up the energy and life that comes only from faith and the gifts God shares. That way, even you can take a licking and keep on ticking" Sounds trite, but it is true. When Bible study and prayer energize your faith, even the cloudy days and cold winters of life will not stop you in your tracks or slow you down.

LOST AND FOUND

✠ ✠ ✠

WE ONCE SPENT A NIGHT in downtown Chicago. Roxanne and I and our daughter Abby had a full day of sightseeing and wonderful pizza, and it was time to turn into our hotel for the night. But the lure of nightlights and reflections was a draw a photographer can't ignore. After the girls were safely in our hotel room for the night, I headed out to take some photos. I got some good shots but also discovered on my return that I had lost my cell phone. I knew the phone was history. There was nothing I could do about it.

A few minutes later, our daughter-in-law, Alli, called from Colorado, asking, "Did you lose your phone?" I knew she was smart but never had a clue she was clairvoyant too! Before I could respond, she said someone found her number on my phone and called to report it was found. She gave the guy who called Roxanne's cell number, and thirty minutes later, I got a call from the young man who found my phone. He was having a dinner meeting nearby and refused any reward, saying he'd just bring it to the hotel when his dinner was done. Just before midnight, he took time to meet me in the lobby before his drive back to the suburbs. As promised, he refused any reward but just smiled as I thanked him and shook his hand.

As I reflect on that, I am amazed by this surprising moment of lost and found. How often do things happen differently from what we might assume or expect? Would I have gone to all the trouble he did? I hope so, but I will never know until I stand in those shoes. How easily he could have ignored a lost phone! How many opportunities do any of us miss because we didn't notice a phone on the street, a tear in someone's eye, or a tremor in a voice? How much this reminds me of the parable of the Good Samaritan, where there were all sorts of good reasons to ignore a wounded traveler, and yet one man didn't.

As we leave Easter's empty tomb, remember our greatest loss has been returned in Jesus's surprising gift of love. His unexpected response to our losses is more important than a cell phone, but isn't it neat that we have so many surprises along the way that give us a chance to remember not to take any of life or living for granted! When are we just strangers? Too busy to notice? And when do we become agents of grace? Think about the opportunities we have when we keep our eyes open to share similar gifts of loving grace with those around us. Isn't that who we are called to be? So, be ready for whoever you might surprise with a find for their loss. And don't ever be afraid to allow someone to be an agent of grace for you!

BUSINESS OR PLEASURE?

✜ ✜ ✜

ON MY WAY TO CHURCH on Sunday mornings, one of my routines was to stop and pick up a Diet Coke, as I can't drink coffee. One Sunday, at about 6:00 a.m., a local convenience store was my stopping place. As I entered, I noticed a new clerk. He was young, with a large, round, shaved head and a half dozen earrings on his left ear. I was forming an opinion (and an attitude), but I wasn't going to let that keep me from my purchase.

The clerk surprised me with a pleasant greeting: "And what brings you out this early on a Sunday? Business or pleasure?" That caught me off guard for sure! But I still wasn't completely awake. I grumbled inwardly about having to participate in a conversation, especially before my caffeine intake. I was tempted, out of frustration at having to talk, to jump all over the softball he had lobbed my way! However, I have learned to listen longer before speaking quickly, as people's questions are often statements rather than a search for an answer. I remained silent. He continued speaking.

He said, "My philosophy is there is no good reason for anyone to be out of bed before ten on a Sunday morning." I broke my silence. I explained I was a pastor and on my way to worship. Then it was his turn to be silent. After a moment, he said, "Well, you must find your work pleasurable." I told him I did, but as I exited the store, I wondered what I had missed. In the silence of my reflection, God drew me closer to him. And I wondered, *Is being a pastor just a business or is it a pleasure?* What a great question!

That caught me off guard and was a tougher question than I thought. I wondered if God had used that young man to make me think about whether or not I enjoyed being a pastor. Was his question a sermon to me? That hit me hard. And so, on the way to work, an unexpected question from a surprising source became that Sunday's sermon to me. My first impulse at the question had been to stop him in his tracks with a clever response, but instead, his question caused me a time of silent reflection, confession, and then prayer that God might indeed help me to enjoy and not just endure my work. I continue to be amazed by the many ways God speaks when I am open to listening. (And by the way, where did your last surprise sermon come from?)

GROWING UP IS HARD TO DO

✠ ✠ ✠

HAVE YOU EVER GOTTEN EXACTLY what you wanted, only to realize you were in over your head or didn't know what to do next? In eighth grade, I was convinced by my best buddy that having a girlfriend was important and really cool. It just so happened there was a girl I would eat lunch with and dance with at our occasional school dances, which was about all an eighth grader could pull off without involving dad and mom. And that was the last thing I wanted them to know about! I was embarrassed to even admit to myself that I had a girlfriend. It just didn't feel normal yet.

Anyway, at the end of the year, it was time for our family to move. Dad was in the army. We had been living in New York and now were headed to Kansas. My girlfriend and her best friend invited me to a farewell picnic in the park across the street from our houses. That sounded OK, but there was no way I would let Mom know, and I was really careful that none of my friends saw me. As I said, it was just an awkward time for me! We had lunch, listened to music, and talked about school. Then came an awkward realization that somehow there needed to be a goodbye.

Uh oh! Panic set in! I was afraid we might have to do something serious like a hug or kiss, and there was no way I could do that! I was in a situation I hadn't thought about, and I didn't know what to do next. Likely, my friends just wanted to say goodbye, and that would be that, but my imagination got the best of me, and I panicked! Suddenly I had an answer. I looked back at the girls and said, "I hear my mom calling! Have to go! Bye!" And I ran home as fast as I could. Not the best solution to an imagined dilemma, but I was, after all, a very immature eighth grader!

As I remember this moment, I am reminded that sometimes when we confront a situation we haven't prepared for (or aren't ready for), we panic or overreact. If I had taken a deep breath, I could have figured out it was no big deal, but that isn't what happened. With hindsight, I realize I was not mature enough for a girlfriend, and I am still embarrassed by such a dorky exit. Forgiveness is a great comfort when we overextend or make stupid mistakes, but sometimes situations that seem important at the time need to be thoughtfully appraised, which can keep us out of trouble in the first place. And yes, growing up is hard to do. And it still is—even now!

SUDDEN GRIEF AND
CERTAIN HEALING

✠ ✠ ✠

MY FIRST YEAR IN MINISTRY was full of surprising moments. In the seminary, I had learned all the right answers, but when I became a pastor, I had to learn about life and figuring out how faith and reality merged. We lived next to a family from church, a couple only about fifteen years older, and we became close. The husband, Dave, became almost like an older brother that I had never had.

One night at 2:00 a.m., his young daughter called hysterically. "Dad's having a heart attack! Mom wants you here right away!" I ran across the street to find paramedics working on him. But he had already died. I had never faced death before and wasn't sure what to do. (I mean really, I had *never* faced any death!) My shock was mingled with knowing I had to be strong.

We prayed, and we talked about how the next day we would begin to plan for what came next. Somehow I held it together, but as soon as I got home, uncontrollable sobbing and wailing came out of my body. I couldn't stop! Our two-year-old daughter just stared and asked my wife, "Why is Daddy crying?"

There was no way I could explain. I couldn't even form words. All I could do was cry. I had never felt such pain.

Despite my inexperience, God guided me through the funeral in a packed church, and we continued to support his wife and family. We visited and offered every help they needed. Even though we had been so close, I gradually saw less and less of his widow, and she quit coming to church. She grew distant and wouldn't return phone calls. No matter what I did, a friendship was lost. Several years later, we had an opportunity to talk, and I pressed hard to find out why we couldn't be friends.

She said, "I thought you loved Dave! You never cried for him! You never showed grief. I can't understand how you didn't show the pain I thought you should feel." There it was! That was it! I explained my grief was so deep that if I had started crying, I never could have done the funeral or been able to talk to the family. If I had started crying the way I wanted, I never would have stopped.

What a lesson that was for me! We have so many expectations of one another, and sometimes those expectations can become burdens and barriers. Grief brings no easy answers, and it opens many other issues that never would have existed. Once the two of us were honest, loving, and open with each other, we understood each other's pain and became friends again. Sometimes it takes great pain to grow in knowing how to love. Sometimes God's gift of healing is slower than we would like. But his healing always comes!

DUCKLING DAUGHTER

✠ ✠ ✠

MY PARENTS FELL IN LOVE with Traverse City, Michigan, which was one of Dad's favorite places to visit when he was on the road. He and Mom found a timeshare, right on the beach of the bay, and had an open invitation for any of their children to come and join them when they were on vacation. Finally, one summer, the stars were aligned, and we were able to get away during one of the weeks they were there.

Our children were quite young, and they instantly fell in love with having a beach right at the back door. One day, the kids were enjoying building sandcastles when our daughter Katie came running with tears in her eyes. "Daddy, there's a baby duck that's hurt. We need to do something!" She took me and showed me a duckling with a damaged eye and injured leg. It wouldn't move. It was likely a victim of the seagulls that aggressively patrolled the beach looking for bread crumbs. She was in tears. This was something she couldn't let go!

My first reaction was this duckling was going to die, but I dared not say that to her! I suggested that we needed to leave the duck alone. Katie was insistent. "Dad, we can't just leave it alone. It will die! Can't we take it into our room and put it in the bathtub?" I wasn't sure Grandma would like a tub full of duck droppings but decided not to allow that to pull Grandma into the drama. I went into my fatherly lecture about letting nature take its course. To be honest, I just didn't want to be bothered. But she was persistent.

As I looked around, trying to figure out how I could steer this conversation in another direction, we noticed two mallards with ducklings swimming behind them. I told Katie we could try something else. "Let's carry the duckling to the water and see if one of the mama ducks might recognize this one." I had doubts, fearing they would just swim away, but we tried anyway. We put the duckling in the water, and then an amazing thing happened. The injured duckling swam toward the closest duck flotilla. They quacked, the little duckling joined the group, and they all swam away—together!

Many of my lessons as a father have been taught to me by my children. And once upon a time, I learned a lesson from a little girl who, at least on this day, decided "It's not about me." Too often, I get preoccupied with my assumptions or "wisdom" and miss the simple acts of love that provide miracles beyond what I could have ever imagined. Sometimes God works in mysterious ways, and this was a reminder that often it is indeed the little ones who find it easier to reach out with love than we who have other things on our minds.

VINCE

✠ ✠ ✠

ONE AFTERNOON, I RECEIVED A phone call from a young mom with a brand-new baby. I had no clue who she was, but she sounded genuine and in need of help. She asked if I might come to visit her and her husband, Vince. He had a brain tumor and was scheduled for surgery in two days. She wondered if I would baptize their little girl before his surgery, just in case. She explained his cancer was incurable, and they weren't certain he would survive the surgery. The next evening, we baptized their little girl.

He had surgery, did remarkably well, and faced a month of recovery followed by radiation. I visited him in the hospital often. The day he began radiation, he told me his wife had taken their daughter and moved out of the house. He didn't know where she had gone. Two weeks later, she served him with divorce papers. He was all alone, dealing with the prognosis of death, the loss of a marriage, and having his new daughter taken away. It had all happened so quickly! Even though the tumor could not be totally removed, he did well. Even though he had lost some of his physical abilities, his recovery was a miracle!

We became good friends, and his old church hired him as a part-time janitor. As he got stronger, he began to work with the youth group as well. No matter what was going on, Vince always had a smile and something positive to share. He always seemed to find joy in what he was doing. Having lost so much, he never displayed anger or bitterness. I know he was lonely and missed his wife and daughter. But he never displayed any bitterness or anger. He was one of the most incredible people I have known. His hair never grew back, but he told me that was not a problem because women prefer men who are bald. That was Vince! Always an upside! And because his faith was so strong, his future was never in doubt.

Four years later, the tumor finally made it clear that he was weeks away from death. We talked about dying and his life, and he was content that he had lived fully and had no regrets. I often thought about Job (whose faith never wandered), and Vince put a face on that character I had known only from a story. He said that Christmas and Easter had changed his life, and he would celebrate in heaven what he couldn't rejoice in on earth. I will never forget what I learned from Vince. And it all was because of a random phone call.

NIGHT TERRORS

✠ ✠ ✠

I ATTENDED A SMALL LUTHERAN junior college in the outskirts of New York City. Most of us were either going to become pastors or teachers. Near the end of my first year, at 2:00 a.m., my roommate woke me up from a deep sleep. He was dressed and yelling at me. "You have to get up!" he said. "There are some guys looking for you down in the lobby. Now!" He looked and sounded scared.

I threw on my sweats and headed down, trying to wake up and having no clue what to expect. The first person I saw was George, a friend from my high school church. He had been expelled from college earlier in the year for having his girlfriend spend the night in his room. (Yes, those were different times!) We weren't that close, and I knew he had been expelled, but I wasn't aware of any of the details. He said he came back to school to beat me up for being the one who told on him and ruining his life. But I hadn't done it!

As I stood in front of a group of guys, I was paralyzed with fear and had no clue how I would get out of it. George kept talking, which gave me time to look for the nearest exit. He said he had spent the whole year plotting this night. He said he hated me for what he thought I had done. I was shaking as I anticipated what was coming next. But I was in for another surprise. He told me when he arrived that night, he and his buddies went out for a beer as they plotted his revenge. At the bar, another guy from our home church (his roommate and best friend) admitted he was the one (not me!) who had turned George in.

He wanted me to hear the whole story! And there we stood. Then he walked toward me while I was still trying to comprehend what was going on. He did what I never would have expected. He asked me to forgive him for all of the hatred he had carried over that past year! I was still trying to figure out if it was just a dream or what. But he hugged me, and we all started crying. (Yeah, college guys in tears— that was weird too!) But what I remember most is that he asked me to forgive him.

How often have I talked behind someone else's back and they never knew? He could have just headed home when he found out the truth, but he felt compelled to confess and ask for me to set him free! I'll never forget that night, and I hope I don't ever forget how important it is to be forgiven. He did more than he needed to do that night, and I am so glad. What a night and what a lesson I learned from George.

DOWNTOWN HAWK

✠ ✠ ✠

ONE OF THE ADVANTAGES ROXANNE and I experienced as our kids grew older was the ability to start having date nights again. One night, we were headed to downtown Kalamazoo for a real meal in a restaurant. Driving down the main street, I looked up at one of the large street signs that hung over the road. Perched on top of the support beam was a large hawk. There was something strange about where he was perched.

As we got closer, I could see that it was using one foot to perch on the sign and the other to hold onto his dinner—a squirrel. I was not sure if that was some sort of prophetic message but didn't spend too much time worrying. However, it did remind me of a similar recent incident I observed from my office window at church: a hawk swooped down and grabbed a squirrel off the playground! (What reminders that life can be tough!)

Obviously, squirrels and hawks aren't people, but they too have to work for their food and don't have as many guarantees in life as they would prefer. Daily there are surprises, hardships, disappointment, and even death. Life is the same whether we are in predator or prey mode. Maybe this isn't the best segue to introduce a season such as Lent, but what a dramatic reminder of the broken world in which we live. Lent reminds us that Jesus has come to bring peace and healing to a world in tension between predator and prey. Lent offers a wonderful forty-day opportunity to remember what God (through Jesus) has done to remedy the losses and weaknesses we endure.

In Lent, we are reminded to practice new disciplines that will better help us to live in the new kingdom that Easter brings. If Easter comes and we miss the point, we have no one to blame but ourselves. If tomorrow comes and we haven't grown through the Lenten blessings of repentance, meditation, prayer, and renewal, we have surrendered a fantastic opportunity to be drawn closer to our God of love. We don't need too many reminders that the world is not as peaceful and perfect as we would like. But Lent helps us remember how God's love prevents Satan from grabbing us as his prey, and instead we are set free to live new lives empowered by faith, hope, and peace!

HERBY CURBY MIRACLE

✛ ✛ ✛

WE NOW HAVE A HERBY Curby to haul trash out to the street. Gone are the days of dented metal trash cans and lids that blow away. One day, I got home and saw that someone tried to run over our Herby Curby. It had a rubber tire mark on the front, was dented and twisted, and the lid didn't fit right. I was not happy! I called, and the trash company promised to deliver a new product by week's end. When I walked out the next morning, I was amazed. Our trash container had bounced back to its original shape. The tire mark was still there, but the damage was undone, and the lid was back in place! I called the company and told them we had witnessed a miracle; Herby was healed. They got a kick of out that and cancelled the order for a replacement.

In the process, I learned two things. First, a Herby Curby is a tough critter! But second, I remembered I need to be careful about overreacting. There was no way to know that Herby would heal himself, but if I had waited a few hours before calling, there would have been no need to call. That reminded me of the many times I have acted impulsively or too quickly when patience and a little time for healing might have changed my perspective.

What if Jesus had fired Peter the first time he had gone off script?

Instead, Jesus's patience allowed Peter to grow into his faith. James and John were damaged goods as they tried to get Jesus to promise them the best seats next to his throne. But Jesus's loving patience kept them around, and they became powerful leaders in the early church.

How often have each of us found that while time might not heal all wounds, it certainly can give us the space we need to calm down and see things in a new light. Sometimes we even find that healing happens best whether we are part of the solution or not. I can get so into my fix-it mode that I often forget some broken things heal better if left alone or surrendered to others, such as this case with a container that is designed to bounce back. What a neat reminder that patience is indeed a virtue! It is sort of like faith; sometimes we just need to let go and see what happens before we react!

SLINGSHOT MOM

✠ ✠ ✠

ONE VISIT TO MOM AND Dad's was particularly memorable, not for what happened but for what didn't. Now I need to set the stage and explain that my mother is not very big, never raises her voice, and is as much a pacifist as anyone I know. She is thin, she is funny, and she never fails to surprise me with something new. Since we only lived about an hour and a half away, we were able to visit quite often. One trip was difficult to forget.

She and Dad knew we were coming, but when we arrived and entered the house, no one was there. The house was empty. I imagined Dad must be working in the garden (his favorite hobby), but where was Mom? I walked through the sunroom into the backyard, and there she was, all 115 pounds of her, standing at the edge of the brick patio. But what was she doing? She had a slingshot, loaded with a marble, and was aiming at a bird feeder that was being emptied by a rather fat squirrel. I couldn't believe it!

I startled her by saying, "Mom! There's a house with windows behind that feeder. What if you miss and break a window?" I couldn't believe Mom would even consider anything so violent as to harm a squirrel or any living thing. Although squirrels are the bane of bird lovers, this was over the top and so out of character. And then came her calm reply and trademark giggle. "Don't worry, I can't even shoot it as far as the feeder!"

I realized she never intended to shoot it! She didn't even have the strength to pull the rubber sling far enough to make a marble fly. This was only a show of force to intimidate the thief on the feeder. Her long-standing battle with her seed-stealing varmints was in full bloom that day! She giggled and put the slingshot away. I should have known that just as a leopard can't change its spots, my mom is incapable of doing physical harm. She just wanted that squirrel to know she was around. (As if the squirrel cared!) But she felt better, and we had a good laugh.

Sometimes we project our own fears and personalities into others and would do better to see Christ first in those we love. (And maybe even in those we don't love!) Mom is always teaching lessons, sometimes by what she does and sometimes by what she doesn't do. St. Paul talks about wearing Christ like a garment. When we learn to do that, even the squirrels know who they are dealing with, and so should I. I made an assumption that in hindsight didn't make sense. Another lesson learned. And another empty feeder. But Mom showed who was boss to the squirrels and to me!

ROBINS IN THE SNOW

✠ ✠ ✠

EVERY WINTER IN MICHIGAN IS unique. One such winter was full of surprises, and one morning something happened I had never seen before. We received a cold front with a driving snow. We weren't the only ones affected. A flock of robins was grounded by the weather. I assume they were heading farther north and had to stop, but as I looked out on the snow-covered church parking lot, there were probably a hundred robins running around. I had never seen a flock of robins running around in a parking lot. I knew they weren't going to find any worms and wondered if they were on the lot because it was warmer than the grass. Whatever was up, it was comical watching so many harbingers of spring running around like chickens with their heads cut off.

Obviously, they too were surprised by the unexpected winter squall. As I reflect on that image, I wonder why it made such an impact. Was it simply a visual reminder of how we often feel and similar scenes that play out every day? Like what happens when we are comfortable in our routine, doing what we normally do, and suddenly a storm or blast of cold wind knocks us down like a flock of birds that can no longer fly? Is that what we must look like to God as we run in circles when surprised by grief or seeking answers where there are none?

We know too well the frantic scurrying that can overwhelm us with panic and fear. It can happen so quickly and it can knock us down just like that storm kept birds from being lifted up from the force of gravity. I just can't get those robins out of my mind and remember how frantic they seemed to be.

But I also remember a day in the life of Jesus when he talked about God's awareness of the life of even the smallest sparrow. And he assured his listeners that if God cared for little birds, he certainly cares for us! That is a powerful reminder that no matter what storm, what fear, or seemingly fruitless search is on our plate, we should not despair. God is with us, and God will keep us safe. We can scurry like chickens with our heads cut off, like robins in the snow, or we can live in the peace that comes from God's love!

GOD'S SURPRISES

✠ ✠ ✠

MANY WONDER ABOUT HOW INVOLVED God really is in the moments of each and every day. How about you? For years, my close friend Jim and I have talked about the surprising ways God works in our lives. He is working on such a story and someday will share it in a more complete way. When he does, there will be more stories than this! Here is a short version of the powerful moment he shared with me. It happened at his cottage on a lake up north.

One winter day, he had been snowmobiling and was walking about a mile from his barn to his home. Several friends stopped and offered him a ride. He was enjoying the walk on a beautiful morning and declined their offers. Then he noticed his boots were not really made for walking and his feet were starting to hurt. He wondered why he had not accepted a ride. Was it pride or something else? Another neighbor stopped and asked if he would like a ride. He thankfully accepted. Casually, he asked the driver, "How's your day going?"

The driver shared he had just been diagnosed with cancer and was in anguish over whether or not to move a frail parent into a care facility. He was worried about making the right decisions. My friend told him to pull over and stop so they could talk. Jim shared he had gone through the same thing fifteen years earlier with his own mom and wrestled with the same issues. They discussed the pros and cons of keeping mom at home or providing round-the-clock care in a facility. In the end, Jim concluded, "You simply have to do the best you can, trust God's guiding, and not look back."

Then the driver then burst into tears. He said, "Just before I got in my car, I had been on my knees, praying to God for a sign to help me know what to do. And then you got in my car!" He said God had answered his prayer. Jim reflected on walking, turning down rides, and then accepting this particular moment to get in a car. Having this opportunity, he realized that God is indeed present and active, even in random events. God doesn't just start life and get out of the way. It is hard to explain, but if it made perfect sense, it wouldn't be called faith. What a difference to see life as a series of random events or see God's presence in every moment! What a difference!

HIDE THE TRANSPONDER?

✠ ✠ ✠

A NEAT GADGET IS THE transponder you put inside the windshield of your car that allows you to pass by toll booths rather than having to wait in stalled traffic. One year, we were on a trip to Minneapolis and stopped at a service plaza in Chicago and bought one. So, even though we live in Michigan, our account is located on the Chicago toll road. Several years ago, I got a notice that our transponder needed to be replaced. I was instructed to put the old one in a box and mail it to Chicago; a new one would be sent back. There was one important instruction, which was to "wrap the transponder in aluminum foil before putting it in a package."

I assumed that was so I was not charged a toll every time the mail truck passed a booth on the way to Chicago. I guess the foil blocks the signal and make the transponder invisible. (This seemed like one of those goofy movies where some knucklehead covers himself in foil to hide from aliens. Ha!) But then came a more sobering thought. How often have I hidden myself (not with foil but in some other way) to make my faith invisible to others? How often have I blocked others through some sort of self-protection or avoidance so that others can't get through to me?

Is my faith visible or something I uncover only when convenient or in panic mode? There is no doubt it's becoming more difficult to be a Christian in a secular culture, especially if we fear ridicule or misunderstanding. We don't like to be labeled as kooks or extremists, so sometimes we hide our light. And yet the first disciples couldn't wait to tell other people how Jesus had changed their lives, and their goal was for God's love to be obvious in how they lived. For many years, Christians sent missionaries any place people didn't know about the saving love of Jesus. Mission work is what caused the church to grow.

We need to be careful that we aren't wrapping our message in foil or hiding our lights under a bushel basket. We need to be careful that we aren't too busy to wash feet or too distracted to hear God's voice calling and comforting in the mayhem of modern and self-absorbed living. In baptism, we say, "Let your light shine!" How might we make that a more comfortable and natural response to the greater lights of Christmas and Easter?

A FERRARI IN DC

✠ ✠ ✠

ONE SUMMER, I WAS IN Washington, DC, for a family gathering. We were walking several blocks from the Mall, and on the other side of the street was a brand-new, shiny Ferrari convertible with the flashiest custom paint job I had ever seen. The car just screamed to be noticed. Two policemen on bikes happened to ride by at the same time. As they pedaled by, they stopped by the car, and I overheard one saying to the other, "Looks like that car needs a speeding ticket!" They laughed and moved on, and I got a chuckle out of that.

Later, I thought about that. Someone didn't just spend a lot of money on a car; they spent even more to make the car unique—and noticed. While it probably says a lot about the personality of the owner, a side effect of that lavish expenditure of funds was that the car was fast, looked fast, and begged to be noticed. Even sitting next to a curb, it looked like it was speeding. (There was no doubt there would be tickets!) That brought another thought.

How often do we intentionally do things to get noticed? Or when do we try to keep under the radar? Now this car could have simply been someone's dream, and they never thought about what others might think. Or it could have been bought with the intent of saying, "Look at me!" When we talk about being a good spouse, a faithful Christian, or a great parent, our motivation is hopefully not about being seen but being a servant. Our motives for faith, hope, and love should never be empowered by a "look at me" desire, and if they are, we are driving the wrong car.

On the other hand, people always notice something about each of us, whether it is our intent or not. So, that leads to a final thought. What do you want them to see when they see you? Is it "look at me" or is it "I am simply being the best servant I can be"? Not only is there a difference in motivation for each answer, but there is a different witness that is shared. How about this: if someone else was pedaling by you at any moment of the day, would they ticket you as a speeder or a servant?

CRAZY HORSE

✝ ✝ ✝

I HAVE BEEN FASCINATED BY the accounts of the original inhabitants of this country, especially the Native Americans of the Wild West. One summer, I read several books about the Lakota Sioux that inspired many lessons all of us would do well to learn and remember. Most impressive to me were some of the books I read about a chief named Crazy Horse.

The history of his people reveals how his and other tribes were destroyed both from within and without. As buffalo herds were decimated and land was forcibly taken away, the Lakota were forced onto reservations with the promise that they would be taken care of forever. They were promised they could hunt, but their horses and guns were taken away. They were promised beef and blankets, but often those were not delivered. Gradually people who had survived off the land became dependent on others and had their identity taken way. After several generations of forced living on reservations, they had no lands to return to and lost skills necessary for survival.

Without going into political arenas with this cautionary tale, I am struck by the similarity of the Garden of Eden, where Adam and Eve were talked out of trusting in God's gifts and sought easier ways to live that were less strenuous and more self-absorbed. It is easy for us to lose sight of what makes each of us special and unique. It is easy to get overwhelmed with the difficulties of life and seek easy ways out. It is tempting to follow shortcuts to living rather than the path of faith and servant love.

When we trust too much in the glitter and power of the world, we become servants to this world and quickly forget how to faithfully live in God's kingdom. Why not utilize some of your leisure and relaxation times to intentionally reflect upon your pathway through life? Are you getting complacent? Have you forgotten the importance and power of faith? Is your life about servant love, or is it about waiting for the world to give you what you deserve? A nation or people can only perish if they forget who they really are and what keeps them alive!

VACATIONS

✠ ✠ ✠

I HAD AN INTERESTING CONVERSATION with a friend about vacations. He asked whether I took vacation in little chunks or all at once. He had been advised by a mentor to take everything all at once, because it takes a week to wind down so that you can relax and enjoy, and a week to gear up at the end for coming back. In the middle is the true vacation. Makes sense! Then I thought about how we go about preparing for living as Christians in our daily lives. Do we prepare in little chunks of worship when it is convenient or just read the Bible once in a while? Or do we do it all at once, all the time, totally immersing ourselves in regular worship, Bible study, prayer, and intentionally reaching out with Jesus's love? Suddenly, a question about the purpose of vacation in my life took on a whole different meaning.

So much planning goes into making sure we find ways to refresh and renew ourselves from our daily routine, but often our faith life becomes more routine than something we plan for and are intentional about. As a pastor, I find I am often so busy doing church work I forget to plan for my own spiritual growth, prayer, and servant love. Despite being surrounded by all the elements of faith, if I don't take time for my own nourishment, it just doesn't happen. How much time do any of us spend at church without actually planning for growth, renewal, and intentional integration of faith into every aspect of our living?

Think about how you plan for vacation, rest, and renewal. Is the same effort given to planning for the nurture of faith? Do you plan for necessary Sabbath rest to better focus on God's love for you? Have you considered how to be Jesus's hands and feet as a parent, a neighbor, or in your vocation? My guess is that just as vacation and summer fun is a necessary break in our routine, so might be the effort to reflect on how our faith life has become too routine and needs a plan for renewal, refreshment, and growth. God has invested so much in us; we might spend more time to regularly plan our response.

OUT OF GAS

✠ ✠ ✠

FULFILLING A LIFELONG DREAM, OUR friends bought a lake cottage. It came with an old pontoon boat. Before they could even enjoy this place that was to be a retirement getaway, the husband died. Several months later, his wife invited us to come over for a meal and a boat ride. She wasn't sure how to start the boat, but I was sure I could (arrogance and ignorance are closely related). She said her grandson had run out of gas the week before and had filled the tank so it should be OK. But I noticed the tank was empty.

Thinking it might have a leak, I added only a few gallons, as I didn't want to fill it if it was leaking. It appeared to be fine. When I got back in the boat, I found the controls were different than any I had ever seen. Even with gas in the tank, it just wouldn't start. A neighbor came and figured it out. As we headed out, he gave us his cell phone number (just in case). We had no problems, and after an hour of driving around lake, we were ready to head back in. Someone asked for one more trip around the lake, so we headed back out. And then the motor stopped. We were out of gas.

I had been so concerned about gas possibly leaking, and I had such difficulty starting the boat, I had forgotten to go back and fill the tank.

Luckily we had that cell phone number of the neighbor. We called. He came out in his boat and towed us back in. There are two issues this brings to mind. First was a neighbor went out of his way to help. Like a Good Samaritan, we appreciate the help of others, but there are so many thoughtful ways we can and should be ready to help others. Keeping eyes open lets us know when help is needed. A neighbor not only gave his number but was willing to help when called. He was thoughtful beyond what he needed to be.

The second issue is easier to accomplish. Simply remember to always keep the tank full! For people of faith, there is never an excuse to run out of gas. God's filling station is always open, and his promise to forgive, lead, and guide are gifts that will empower every moment of our lives. Worship, Bible study, and prayer are just some of the ways we keep our tanks full. Too often, we are easily distracted by obsessions, fear, or grief, and our tanks can get pretty empty. But when we keep filling our living with God's gifts of grace, we will never be surprised in the middle of a journey. The life lessons I learned that day weren't new but are often forgotten: Be a neighbor! And keep your tank full!

FOLLOWING SHADOWS

✠ ✠ ✠

I USUALLY WALK AROUND SIX in the morning, which means that in Michigan, for much of the year, I walk in the dark. But one of the joys of this time is the peace and quiet and closeness I feel with God, and sometimes when it is darkest, it is easier to see the light! And so this has become a favorite time of meditation and prayer. (And surprise.) Earlier one winter, when it was quite dark and foggy, I came upon a man who was standing still and facing away from me. I said good morning, and he responded in kind. As I passed, I noticed two smaller shapes about twenty feet in front of me. (His dogs.) Thinking that I might be uncertain about dogs, he told me that they were good dogs and would not bother me.

As I walked past him, his dogs heard him speaking. And then a funny thing happened. As I walked past the dogs, they started following *me*! I noticed them moving with me and stopped before we got too far down the path. Laughing, I turned back to him and said, "I think they are confused." He agreed, saying his oldest dog was pretty blind. I waited for him to catch up so his dogs would follow him rather than me. That was one of those early-morning moments that I so enjoy and am often surprised by. I never know what each new day will bring, but this was the dogs' gift to me!

I thought about how often we are like those dogs. We don't always see as well as we should and are creatures of habit so that, in the darkness, we do what we are conditioned to do. The dogs heard a familiar voice, saw a shape, and started following the wrong master. Think about how easily and how often we do the same. Blinded by grief or anger, or cast into the darkness of fear, depression, or death, we can easily forget who we are called to follow and what steps will lead us safely home. We hear sounds that are temptingly familiar, and if we don't pay attention, we can be led astray. Sometimes we are so busy we don't even notice that the shapes and sounds around us aren't really that familiar. This is how bass get caught, dogs get confused, and we can be led astray. Pay attention in the shadows and remember who you are called to follow.

REMEMBER WHOSE YOU ARE

✛ ✛ ✛

WE LIVE IN A CONFUSING world. We live in a time of cultural relativism, where judgments as to what is right or wrong are based on the mood of the times rather than core principles of one's existence. My mother had a different approach. She never told me what I should or shouldn't do when I went out with friends during my high school years. Instead, her words as I headed out the door were always the same. "Remember whose you are!"

Even more amazing is that I knew what she meant. When I thought about what the priorities of faith and family were and balanced that against what seemed right or felt good at the moment, it was not that I always made the best decisions, but I knew (deep in my heart) what those decisions should be. I don't have to enumerate all the issues dealing with morality and daily choices, but we all know that each issue is faced from various possible perspectives.

Some make choices based on what feels good at the moment. Some are guided by peer pressure. Some simply follow rules given by others. Some are paralyzed because they can't make any decision. There is no doubt that my grandparents' entire life was based on their life of faith. And that is where my parents learned their values. We have grown up in a world with many more distractions, choices, and diversions, and often, even in my chosen vocation, the choices are tough. My mom had it right, and her four-word sermon was always the same. "Remember whose you are!"

That is why Israel was given commandments and Jesus told disciples to love! As God's children, that is who we are—God's family. Love for God and those around us is the first and only reason we should do anything. When we remember whose we are, it no longer is my life, my possessions, my feelings, or my needs but God's life, God's gifts, and opportunities God has given me for a reason. Think about it! Does that not change your focus and your response to each and every moment of your living? (And help you as a parent, grandparent, or friend?) Remember God's grace, but also remember whose you are! We won't always get it perfect, but at least we'll have a good start!

GRANDPA WAS GROUNDED

✛ ✛ ✛

THERE ARE MANY DISAPPOINTMENTS IN life—many moments we can't control and days that don't turn out the way we wish. How often has there been a path in the road, and while you wanted to go right, you were forced to go left? And we all understand that once we are headed on a certain path (whether by choice, chance, or someone else's decision), we can't go back. Then we get frustrated or depressed or feel cheated. No one wants to live with a chip on the shoulder, but sometimes don't you wish you could wave a magic wand and get exactly what you think you need?

I am reminded of a story my grandfather told. He was a missionary in the Philippines, and one day he planned to take a plane ride from one island to another. As he started to board the plane he had chosen (in the early 1950s in the Philippines, there weren't a lot of choices), he was asked to get off the plane. Someone else wanted his seat and was in a big hurry. That meant a long delay for Grandpa and not being able to accomplish what he hoped for. But he gave up his seat and simply made new plans.

Later on, he would learn that this first plane never arrived at its destination but went down in the ocean, with all lives lost. What do you make of that? Was it simple chance or divine intervention? Does it really matter? The bottom line is that we live in a broken world. Things don't always work out the way we would like, and sometimes our need to control is very shortsighted, and it is impossible to know for certain what the long-term ramifications of our choices might be.

Faith is all about living with what we can't control and accepting the loving presence of a God who will be with us no matter what. While we are never certain of tomorrow's surprises, how great to be gifted with faith! Sometimes a fork in the road is not as important as how we walk after we take that turn. Next time you want to complain about what you didn't get or the unexpected journey you were forced to take, maybe it would make more sense to celebrate the unexpected and undeserved surprises God has given!

DOWNSIZING

✛ ✛ ✛

AFTER MY FATHER DIED, WE all helped our mom downsize, as she decided to move out of their condo and into a smaller apartment. It caused me to look at the stuff I had collected over the years. What did I really need, and what did I want to do to make future decisions easier for my family? All of us spend a lifetime of collecting, whether we intend to or not. There are obvious things like furniture, books, photos, appliances, pets, art, utensils, and all sorts of other sundry items. We know we can't take them with us, but we so much enjoy the company and surroundings that give life its color and warmth.

Our stuff is so much an extension of our personalities, but it also can control our living. Think of how difficult it is to let go of something that has been around for many years. A favorite piece of art, an extra camera, projects you someday will get to, or an antique piece of furniture. And there are the more powerful gifts of life like our children and our memories. How difficult it is to let those out of our sight! And yet we also spend a lifetime learning to let go.

Faithful living is about learning to keep from overfilling our backpacks. The heaviness of too much stuff can become a weight that prevents us from moving forward—or at all. Memories are like that, whether good or bad. Who can surrender the memory of a game-winning homerun, the birth of a first child, or the loss of our greatest love? And how does that often cause some to never gather or even love, as the fear of loss is greater than some want to handle? What a sad condition indeed. But in letting go, there is a wonderful opportunity to celebrate the gifts that have been part of our surroundings and entrust our next steps to God's care rather than our control.

I am not advocating emptying our lives of stuff or turning our backs on painful losses or incredible joy but rather am reminded of the importance of keeping perspective. Early Christians had such a difficult life that heaven was a goal they couldn't wait for. We have such full lives we don't want to think about heaven at all! Somewhere in between is where faith calls us to live. This is not an answer but a reminder of the priorities of life. With my future secure, it changes how I look at present stuff.

GRANDMA AND GRANDPA

✠ ✠ ✠

MY GRANDPARENTS LIVED IN ST. Joseph, Missouri. It was the home of the Pony Express. It was full of stockyards and railyards, and I loved them as much as I loved anyone. We only saw them once a year at the most, but when we did, we would get to stay with them for a whole week. Grandma could bake chicken and coffee cake like no one else! Grandpa would take us fishing for catfish and let us play in the seed house where he was a manager. They had an old house with a fruit cellar and a clothes chute big enough to hide in. They had a pigeon coop and an old garage with a dirt floor, which were great areas to play cowboys and Indians. (Yes. I grew up in a different age.)

The only problem was (except for our best Christmas ever!) that we always went in the summer. And it was always really hot. I mean, hot! Our little bedroom upstairs with no fan was a terrible place to sleep due to the heat. Church and Sunday school were also part of the routine (but that was OK because it was part of our routine every week anyway). The ushers gave us little cardboard fans with a picture of Jesus on one side and the name of a funeral home on the other. We would spend the entire worship service fanning ourselves, trying to cool off. However, one summer we happened to be there during vacation Bible school.

That meant the whole week was spent in a hot church basement with a bunch of kids we didn't know.

At least Grandma was there, because she played the piano and seemed to be in charge, so we felt safe. Those were the days of Kool-Aid and flannel graphs. And if we were lucky, a filmstrip rather than someone just reading a story. (You can ask someone old like me what that means.) Anyway, that vacation seemed more like work than fun, for a hot church basement was an uncomfortable place to be when we would rather be fishing or playing in the orchard behind Grandpa and Grandma's house.

But as I remember the loving commitment of my grandparents to keep our priorities straight, I understand why that time was indeed special and how I probably gained more than I gave up. How fortunate I am to have a family who always kept priorities straight—even when it was hot!

ANGELS IN OUR MIDST

✛ ✛ ✛

WHEN MY WIFE, SUZIE, DISCOVERED she was dying of cancer, our life changed. Her incredibly difficult journey was marked by courage, grace, and love. To be honest, she did better than I did. My struggle with being a husband, father, and pastor was not always pretty. We had three young children who were going to grow up without their mother. There was no easy way to wrestle with the reality of what we were up against. Several months into that struggle, a raspy-voiced, seventy-year-old woman came into my church office one morning. She said, "My name is Gloria. I am a psychiatric social worker. I have worked seven days a week for forty years and decided it was time to retire. I need to join a congregation, and I want to serve by sharing the gifts of my experience."

She weekly met with our youth minister and me to assist with difficult people issues and make suggestions for how to support those in crisis. Along the way, I asked if she would serve as a sounding board for me. I wondered if she would keep an eye on me and make sure I was being realistic in dealing with my wife's illness and listen to me when I had no one else to talk to. I had a therapist already, but Gloria watched me on a more daily basis, read my articles, heard my sermons, and watched how I functioned (or didn't). She agreed and for several years became a strength in the journey that was thrust upon me.

Along the way, she causally mentioned that she had a large tumor in her lung, which was inoperable because of advanced heart disease. As the tumor had not grown for twenty-five years, she chose not to undergo any treatment. She was realistic and at peace. We became good friends, and she was a powerful source of strength for a journey I had no experience with. We talked several times a week, and her presence brought insight and peace into my life.

Soon after my wife died, Gloria told me that her lung tumor had begun growing again, and she had only a few months to live. Now the tables were turned. She had no family, so I became the one who listened to and supported her in her journey home. As I think back on the timing of her appearance and also her departure from our lives, I cannot believe anything else than God sent her into our lives for a reason. My feeling is that angels come in many shapes and sizes, but there is no doubt that it is exactly who she was.

COCO AND WINNIE

✛ ✛ ✛

OUR DOGS KEEP LIFE INTERESTING. Coconut is getting old and deaf. Winston is younger but is a beagle. (Need I say more?) Sometimes we don't know whether to laugh or be frustrated. Their newest first was a daring nighttime escape from the fenced-in backyard. When we called them to come in, they didn't. We decided if they wanted to spend the night in the yard, so be it! Who wants to plead at midnight with a dog who is deaf and another who pretends to be?

In the morning, Roxanne heard Winnie whining at the front door. She let him in but couldn't figure out how he had gotten there. I went out to look for Coco and found her limping down the street. She was bleeding from her nails that were worn down. Both dogs slept the entire day. (I guess they are both too old for all-nighters!) I finally found their escape route, through a loose board in our privacy fence where rabbits enter and leave. It was pushed away from the nails. I assume Winston forced his way out, and Coconut blindly followed. There was no way to get back in. They likely kept coming back to the house, but with no way to get in, they just wandered all night.

This reminds me how each day is a new learning experience. Often we encounter surprises (usually more serious than runaway dogs).

Sometimes rabbits need to be chased, and often we can't go back through a doorway we have opened. Life is like that. Sometimes we just have to go with the flow and see what comes next. And isn't that what faith is all about? A dog has faith that if they go to their familiar place, they will eventually be petted and fed. Because that is true, our dogs came home, and we could welcome them back.

I need to remember how that works for me. Faith is knowing that God's love is my true home. No matter how lost or confused I am, he is waiting to welcome me home with his loving embrace. Fear and worry accomplish nothing. Faith is knowing if I knock, the door will be opened, and everything I need is already waiting. What I have learned again is that my dogs do their version of faith better than I do. It hurts to say I had to learn something from my dogs, but I did. Faith makes any journey more successful and always brings peace.

SURPRISES

✠ ✠ ✠

MY WIFE, SUZIE, DECIDED ON a surprise fortieth birthday party for me. She did all of the planning, without me every having any inkling of what she was up to. It happened on Saturday, my normal grass-cutting day. I finished the grass at about the time I usually did. When I was heading upstairs for a shower, she pushed me to make it quick. I thought nothing more about it, but when I came downstairs, I was overwhelmed by seeing our backyard full of friends who immediately shouted, "Surprise!" Pretty neat, huh? She really pulled it off. I was speechless and caught completely off guard but for a different reason.

Two days earlier, we had gotten the life-changing news that she had incurable, terminal cancer. She and I were still trying to sort through that news, which had no good prognosis. We hadn't figured out how to tell our three children. I was so overwhelmed with sadness I had forgotten it was my birthday. But Suzie decided not to make any changes to our routine. The real surprise was we were living with a different reality than our friends. We were preparing for a death while they were joyfully celebrating life. Without knowing it, they helped us celebrate life as well! Several weeks later, they all would know, when we were ready to talk about it.

I still marvel at the selfless love and confident faith of my wife, who didn't want her condition to interfere with a day that she thought was worthy of joy. It should have been no surprise to me, but that was how she spent the next two years of her struggle with cancer. Every day was special, as she decided the surprise of cancer would not be more powerful than the greater daily gifts of family, faith, hope, and love. She gave me and everyone who knew us more of a birthday gift than anyone has ever been given. And such a surprise response to the world's greatest fear became the parable in our lives for how faith in the miracle of Easter can surprise even the fear of death.

Just as Jesus caught the world off guard with an empty tomb on Easter, she surprised us with her ability to let that powerful gift bring daily miracles into her struggle—and ours today!

DRIVER'S LICENSE PHOTO

✠ ✠ ✠

THIS IS EMBARRASSING. IT'S ABOUT my driver's license photo, which looks like a mug shot from *America's Most Wanted*. My passport photo is worse! It is difficult when one doesn't have a lot to work with anyway, but those types of photos can damage any self-confidence that one might attempt. Even worse are the new rules: "No glasses and no smiling." As I look at such unflattering photos that make me look like a demented old man, I don't know what to say or feel.

But it also encouraged me to consider something more important. All of us, even though we don't always think about it and seldom admit it, really do care about what we look like. That is why we buy the clothes we do, cut or color our hair the way we do, and take so much time picking out glasses we have to wear. That is also why we have mirrors, so that we at least have some control over what others see. That is all well and good.

But if we can get beyond the *beauty is only skin deep* phase, it is even more important to ask ourselves, What do others *know* about me, *think* about me, or *say* about me? That is more important than what my face appears to be. Last year in one of his sermons, a pastor friend said the most important thing any of us should be willing to share with someone when they ask who we are is "I am a Christian!" Not where I work, or how many kids I have, or who I am married to. Simply "I am a Christian." And since most of the impressions that others get from us are not from what we say but how we live, this becomes even more of an issue.

Every Christmas, we celebrate the birth of a baby who has indeed changed our lives forever. Our response to the Christmas miracle ought to be that Jesus is the beauty, joy, and peace in my life. And when that gift is opened in how I live, others will see Jesus rather than just me. The net result of that is that if people like my wife or children or friends know by how I treat them that Jesus really has impacted my life, that is what they will see in me, rather than a driver's license image that might reflect something different from who I really am. So, what do you want to look like?

PEARS

✠ ✠ ✠

WE ALL HAVE STORIES ABOUT how little children surprise us when least expected. Several years ago, our grandson Jack caught his parents off guard in such a moment. They were sitting, beginning to eat, and Jack shouted, "Pears! Pears!"

Chris and Courtney looked at each other, confused. They replied, "We're sorry, Jack, but we don't have pears tonight."

He persisted, "Pears! Please! Pears!" They looked at each other again.

Then they suddenly understood. He was asking for prayers! They had forgotten to pray. How often have any of you been in a situation where you were being such an adult! So mature! And a child became the teacher, and you became the student. It happens more often than we like to admit. As adults, we make life so complicated and are so busy that often we fail to see the single tree in a massive forest.

We are so overwhelmed with our complicated lives that we often miss the simple, small voice that calls us back to reality. Youngsters have a way of cutting through all the nonsense of the adult world with their simple view. Where we see shadows, they see black or white. We see complexity, and they see simplicity. We're burdened by experience, and they visit each new moment for the first time. We have so much to learn from our little ones! And we have so much we would do well to forget!

Do you realize this was part of God's plan as he showed up in a manger as a baby, rather than as an adult with a fancy robe and jewel-bedecked throne? Children are so easy to take for granted, as are those who are different from us. Over and over again, Jesus reminded his disciples that loving God means loving all of his children. And sometimes even a child or someone we might overlook can become God's example of faith for you and me.

We have to learn from the faith of inexperience and humble trust. There is something in the simple hug and love of a child that we too easily forget. There is something in the black-and-white perspective of an infant that we would do well to remember. Don't forget that Jesus came as a baby so that all the smart and powerful adults would forget that what they think is important is not as important as what we knew as babies—loving trust. It is no more simple or complicated than that. And it started with a baby.

SODA POP IN THE OVEN

✠ ✠ ✠

MY UNCLE CHARLIE WAS A special mentor in my life. He was bigger than life and always full of joy, faith, hope, and love. And he was not shy about sharing advice. When I was five, we visited him in Florida, where he was serving as a pastor in his first church. In later years, he loved to remind me of something that happened when we visited. He told me (which I don't remember) that I hid a bottle of 7UP in the oven, and when Aunt Audrey turned on the oven to heat it for a Sunday-morning dinner, the bottle exploded! (Who me?)

Since his death, I often think of my uncle Charlie. I wonder why he told me that story so often, as he never shared anything without it having a purpose. I don't remember that event at all but can't stop thinking about it.

As a kid, I did have a devious streak (colored by selfishness) and have a sneaky feeling I likely hid that bottle of soda in the oven so my little brother wouldn't find it. That way, I would have it all to myself. This is just conjecture, but it makes sense. Why else would I have done that? As I wonder if that was the reason or not, I think about why Uncle Charlie told me that story so often, when there are hundreds of other shared experiences we could have discussed.

This is pure speculation, but I might have an answer. I wonder if it was his gentle way of reminding me that even though I was an adorable and funny little kid, I could also be selfish. Maybe this was his gift of holding a mirror in front of me, and now, even after his earthly death, he is able to help me keep my priorities straight and think about what I do, why I do it, and what my motives should never be.

It is always a danger to put words into someone else's mouth or motives into their heart when they cannot defend themselves, but I have a feeling Uncle Charlie could never pass up an opportunity to help me grow (just as he did for everyone he ever touched). His love changed my life. He lifted me up in my times of grief, encouraged me in my efforts of writing, and was my sounding board in times when ministry was too intense. And, like the parables Jesus also told, he always shared stories to make sure I paid attention to what was important. Why else remember a bottle of soda pop in the oven? What a wonderful God we have who places Uncle Charlies in our lives!

SNOW ANGELS

✟ ✟ ✟

YEARS AGO, WHEN MY YOUNGEST daughter, Abby, was still in preschool, we had a wonderful snowfall several days after Christmas. There is nothing more exciting for a child than fresh snow, especially when the joy of Christmas morning is still bubbling away. She begged to go outside to play. Once dressed in snowsuit, gloves, cap, and boots, she ran and immediately lay on her back in the snow. She started swinging arms and legs back and forth. We laughed as we watched her making a snow angel! And it was an energetic one at that.

As I watched more closely, I saw her lips moving and realized she was talking. I didn't want to distract her, so I quietly slid open the back door only to hear her saying, over and over again, "Don't be afraid! Don't be afraid!" I told Roxanne what our daughter was saying. At first, it didn't click, but then we both got it. She was repeating the words of the angels to the shepherds, "Don't be afraid!"

The Christmas story had energized her mind. She wasn't just making a snow angel; she *was* the Christmas angel. "Don't be afraid! Don't be afraid!" It reminded me that children really do listen and remember. And that is how the Christmas story touched her heart. "Don't be afraid!"

When I was a kid, we just made snow angels so we could stand back and look at what we had created. Her acting career started early, as she had become an angel in the snow, and her role was to repeat the good news of Christmas. "Don't be afraid!" What better message is there than "Don't be afraid"? Whether to shepherds near Bethlehem, to a little girl in church on Christmas Eve, or the world in which we live today, what better message is there than "Don't be afraid! Don't be afraid!"? Because a baby was born in Bethlehem, there is nothing that can ever separate us from God's love. And that love brings peace to any conflict or pain or fear. "Don't be afraid!" What good news! And what a great memory for me!

RUINING A CHRISTMAS GIFT

✠ ✠ ✠

IT IS AMAZING HOW OFTEN an offhand and critical comment can become so hurtful to someone else. Why are we often better at hurting than helping?

When my son, Chris, was in middle school, he spent the fall working for our neighbors by walking dogs, cutting grass, and bringing in mail when they were on vacation. He was quite generous with Christmas gifts that year, having a plan and budget for what he wanted to share. Knowing my love of cooking, he bought me a cast-iron pot rack to hang from the ceiling over our kitchen island.

It was quite a surprise and exactly what I would have loved to have, but there was no way there would be room for it with an eight-foot ceiling. Without thinking, my first reaction was "This won't work in our kitchen."

What a fool I can be! Why would love ever be replaced with a comment that, although practical, could bring pain to someone I love? How often do we hurt others when that might not have been our intent? Immediately I realized what I had done. First responses are often best kept unspoken, but that isn't always my way. For a father to hurt a child in such a way is more than embarrassing and painful. It is obviously a memory impossible to forget. I immediately apologized to Chris, explaining it was a wonderful gift. But that should have been my first word and not one of saving face.

Why is it that we sometimes hurt the people we love the most, or embarrass ourselves because we are so quick to criticize the impractical or poor choices of others? What happens that we speak before we think, or fail to recognize that words can wound as painfully as any weapon?

Sometimes we are smarter than those around us, and sometimes we are right and they are wrong. But how can it ever be helpful to hurt rather than help—or cause pain rather than heal? A principle taught to physicians is "First, do no harm." I like that! It sounds a lot like Jesus's words about loving as we have been loved. Washing feet is better than pointing out the fact that they are dirty. Love is not only a gift for me but the first gift I am called to share!

CAN I PAY YOU NOT TO CRY?

✛ ✛ ✛

MANY YEARS AGO, TWO LITTLE boys were let loose to play. My brother and I were always ready for new adventures, and this would be an interesting one. Our dad was an officer in the army, and we lived in Germany about fifteen years after the war. Our family was on a vacation in Bavaria, where, for the first time ever, we stayed in a real hotel!

Dad and Mom were busy with the girls and felt it was OK for us to go outside and let off some steam—which we did, as only little boys can do. It didn't take long before we found a few other boys who also were anxious to get outside, and we jointed them. They were throwing cobblestones against a vacant building, and we joined the fun. It was a grand idea until a cobblestone bounced back and hit my little brother in the head!

Donny started bleeding. He was crying. I grabbed his hand and ran back to the hotel to find Mom! Little boys always look for Mom when they are hurt! Running through the lobby, a lady stopped us and said to Don, "Little boy, if I give you a quarter, will you stop crying?" I was confused. How would money stop bleeding or pain? Plus, she didn't understand little boys never cry unless they are really hurt! Ignoring the lady in the lobby, we ran to Mom, and as she always did, she became the loving nurse who took care of my brother.

That lady in the lobby's offer of money was never forgotten. How typical to seek a remedy for what makes us uncomfortable and assume that what we value most will be valued by others. Or that change can be bought if the price is right. Happiness, an end to tears, peace, healing, respect—doesn't everything have a price?

We live in a broken world where little boys make mistakes and adults are sometimes clueless. And isn't that the reason God filled a Bethlehem manger with a baby? A helpless child is the gift he shared with an entire world. This baby would grow to be the healer for all wounds and the gift that would end tears of pain. He would pay the price to bring peace. Who could ever imagine a better plan for healing than that? So, whether wounded by a cobblestone or clueless when it comes to how to end our tears, the good news is that a baby in a manger has come to fix what we cannot and heal what is broken. And that is the only gift that will bring true joy and peace!

TRAPPED IN A STORM

✠ ✠ ✠

MY FRESHMAN YEAR OF HIGH school, we lived in Kansas City, Missouri. Dad was in Vietnam, as part of the first big troop buildup of the war. He and Mom decided we should live close to relatives just in case something happened to Dad. When he flew out of Fort Riley with his battalion, we headed for a rented house in a city we had never lived in before.

There were no school buses, so Mom would drop me off at high school in the morning, and I would make the mile-and-a-half walk every afternoon, as she was busy rounding up four siblings from their schools. The walk was OK in good weather, but one day I was about halfway home, and I heard the wail of tornado sirens starting to blare. I looked toward the west, where the sky was darkest, and saw a funnel starting to dip from a black cloud bank on the horizon.

It was likely at least ten miles away but moving quickly and definitively a tornado. I have never been so scared! Sirens were still wailing, and I didn't know which way to run. We had just moved into town. I didn't know the neighborhood, and no one was outside. I was trapped!

I heard a horn honk, and there on the other side of the road was

Mom! Somehow she had managed to get her four youngest out of school early, and she came looking for me. I don't know how she figured out where I might be on my walk home, but there she was at just the right place and certainly the right time! We got home, pulled into the garage, and just then, hail started falling, and the wind picked up. I took a peak outside before we headed into the basement and saw the funnel starting to lift back up into the clouds as it passed over our house. We were safe!

Once upon a time, on the Sea of Galilee, Jesus's disciples were caught by a sudden storm as Jesus was asleep in the back of the boat. When they woke him up, he calmed the wind and waves and ended the drama of the storm. He then reminded his friends that despite their concerns, he had always been close by. He shared they needed to learn to quit worrying about everything they couldn't control and have faith in his love for them.

That lesson in faith became even more important when they faced another storm at the foot of Calvary's cross. Easter made it clear, then and now, that God is close and will never let us go. My mom gave me similar relief one day when I thought I was trapped. I should have had faith she would look for me! Faith is surrender to a love that never lets us down. And remember that faith always brings peace!

ERNIE THE ROOFER

✝ ✝ ✝

ONE OF THE MORE INTERESTING characters in my early ministry was a Polish roofer. Toledo was full of hardworking, blue-collar, salt of the earth people. Ernie was one of those. He was a union man, usually working on large commercial buildings. He was built like a fireplug, could probably bend iron rods with little effort, and had a five o'clock shadow by 8:00 a.m. His fingers were permanently discolored by tar, and he once fell forty feet down an elevator shaft without being injured.

He was a Sunday regular and always said hello but never more than that. I sensed he was not comfortable with me as his pastor but never could figure out why. It wasn't something that I worried about, but it kept us at a distance from each other. Over the years, he was gradually more approachable but never very friendly. There was never any overt hostility, but I was paranoid enough to assume he was watching and waiting for me to fail. As time went on, I just quit worrying about whether he would run me out of town or not.

One year, he was elected chairman of our board of elders, so we had to work closely and deal with many issues concerning people and ministry. After one long meeting, he asked if he could have a word with me in private. I wondered if it would be in a dark alley and whether I would ever see my wife and kids again! So after everyone left, he said, "Pastor, before you even came here, I had decided I didn't like you. You were too young, I knew you wouldn't do a good job, and you went to the wrong seminary. Before I knew you, I think I even hated you."

Then came the kicker, as he continued, "Now I need you to know that I love you like a son." He embraced me and said, "I am glad you are our pastor." I never found out all that was involved or what led up to that, but I wasn't going to risk losing such a moment. To see this man, who was literally as tough as nails, being willing to confess his past and his present unconditional support was a moment like out of a movie! Life is full of surprises.

What I learned from this is sometimes we simply need to be patient, trust in God's presence, and allow his Spirit to work little miracles like that. If either of us had pushed too hard early on, neither of us would have found the peace that only Christ can bring. This was a wonderful lesson that caught me by surprise and was brought to me by Ernie the roofer.

LESSONS FROM MY SON

✠ ✠ ✠

BEFORE I HAD CHILDREN, THERE was no way to understand how important they would become in my life or how our relationships would change over the years. One Christmas Eve in Toledo, I went to church early. My wife, Suzie, got there late and said our two-year-old, Mark, had pulled the Christmas tree down on himself! Two-year-olds bring unexpected memories.

Years later, having endured the death of his mother and his dad getting remarried, Mark prepared for his own marriage. He had just graduated from college, and he and his bride-to-be had all the planning completed. They planned to get married in the beautiful chapel at Valparaiso University, where they had gone to school. They wanted me to perform the ceremony.

We were all set but were blindsided by tragedy two weeks before the wedding. My daughter died. Katie and Mark were only two years apart in age and had always been the best of friends. Her death was sudden and unexpected and rocked our world with grief. We struggled through the funeral and then had to deal with his wedding. He insisted I still needed to be the one to perform the wedding. I wasn't sure I could and tried to back out. He was firm with me, saying, "Dad, I need you to do our wedding."

With help from a loving God, we were able to celebrate that special night. I realize now what I didn't know then. He needed his dad to be close as he endured a terrible loss *and* was filled with the joy of his marriage. He wasn't being selfish but embracing our love. And I know now how much it meant for me to have my son stand with me as well, just as his brother Chris had driven to with me to Chicago a week before to help plan the funeral of his sister.

As our children become adults, they become more like friends. Ten years later, Mark and his wife had the opportunity to live in Switzerland for a year. I traveled to visit them in a place I had never been. He and Alli ferried me throughout the country and even into Italy and France for a special family trip I will never forget. He had researched and planned all our places to stay and translated the menus I could not read.

In a way, he was doing for me what I had done when he was a child and we traveled. He was like a parent, making sure I was taken care of, as love always makes certain that will happen. Another stage and another reminder of how important our children are in our lives. As I reflect upon God's gifts in my life and how my relationships with my children change and grow, I have another insight into the wisdom of God's creative love. His gifts keep opening in new and more complete ways. His love never ends!

ABOUT THE AUTHOR

✠ ✠ ✠

TIM SEEBER GREW UP IN an Army family, living in Japan, Germany, and throughout the United States. He is a Lutheran pastor, married, and the father of four children. He has served parishes in Florida, Ohio and Michigan, and enjoys photography, sports, reading, writing, and cooking.

Printed in the United States
by Baker & Taylor Publisher Services